Underst

the Unemployed

Understanding the Unemployed

THE PSYCHOLOGICAL EFFECTS OF UNEMPLOYMENT

JOHN HAYES

AND

PETER NUTMAN

TAVISTOCK PUBLICATIONS
LONDON AND NEW YORK

First published in 1981 by
Tavistock Publications Ltd
11 New Fetter Lane, London EC4P 4EE
Published in the USA by
Tavistock Publications
in association with Methuen, Inc.
733 Third Avenue, New York, NY 10017
© 1981 John Hayes and Peter Nutman
Photoset by Rowland Phototypesetting Ltd
Bury St Edmunds, Suffolk
Printed in Great Britain by
Richard Clay (The Chaucer Press) Ltd
Bungay, Suffolk

British Library Cataloguing in Publication Data

Hayes, John
Understanding the unemployed.
1. Unemployed – Psychological aspects
I. Title II. Nutman, Peter
331.1'37   HD5708

ISBN 0-422-77830-3 Pbk

Contents

To Ann and Mercia
and our children
Kel, Tom,
Sarah, Jonathan.

Preface

'A man willing to work, and unable to find work, is perhaps the
saddest sight that fortune's inequality exhibits under this sun.'

THOMAS CARLYLE, *Chartism*, 1839

There is an increasing interest in and concern about the consequences of unemployment for the individual. It now appears
that the recent higher levels of unemployment may not be a short-
term phenomenon but an enduring feature of western society.

Recent publications on unemployment have tended to ignore
the individual and focus attention on the broader social, economic, and political issues. This book takes a different perspective
and examines how the individual reacts to and copes with this
dramatic and fundamental transition. The literature in this area is
sparse and disorganized. In the process of researching the psychological effects of unemployment we found, after a computer
assisted literature search in 1979, fewer than 200 articles and
theses on the subject. These and more recent material, together
with some of our own findings from more than forty interviews,
are drawn together in an attempt to produce a coherent framework for analysing the psychological effects of unemployment.

Unemployment, in our work-oriented society, has many consequences that may remain relatively hidden while the problem
is small. However, as more and more people are deprived of the
opportunity to work the psycho-social implications of unemployment become more evident.

In writing this book we have found it difficult to express
adequately what unemployment means for many people. Even
such phrases as 'sullen and despondent acceptance' hide many of
the emotions and feelings we encountered when interviewing
the unemployed. Without at least some empathetic understanding of what lies behind such phrases it is difficult to appreciate
the extent and intensity of the various psychological states we
have tried to describe.

The consequences of unemployment for the individual demand

the attention of a broad spectrum of people throughout society such as social workers, educationalists, members of the medical profession and managers involved in redundancy programmes and the employment of those who have been unemployed. If these people are to perform their roles effectively they require an understanding of the psychological effects of unemployment.

We hope such people, and others concerned with the problems of unemployment, will find this book useful.

John Hayes
Peter Nutman
February 1981

1 The nature of the problem

*'People should keep unemployment figures in perspective. . . .
There is an enormous obsession with unemployment. It is all too
easy to talk oneself into a position of gloom and despondency.'*

SIR JOHN EDEN, Minister for Industry, speaking at
Sheffield, England, 27 September 1971

Many of the recent publications on unemployment have tended
to ignore the individual. They have focused on the broader social,
economic, and political issues and have tended to refer to the
individual as if he or she were merely an anonymous statistic.
This view of the unemployed individual as a unit of statistical
data is not lost on those who are unemployed. It has been a
recurring feature of our interviews with unemployed people, and
commonly mentioned in the case studies of other writers, for the
unemployed to describe their predicament within such a statistical
framework. This was expressed implicitly by one person when
she reported her recent redundancy by saying, 'I've just been
added to the list', and explicitly by another who said, 'I've just
been made a statistic.'

This book is an attempt to redress the balance by placing the
individual at the centre of the picture. In examining unemployment from the perspective of a psycho-social transition, the book
considers the variety of ways in which individuals react to and
cope with premature involuntary job loss.

Whilst concurring with Kurt Lewin's argument that, 'even if
all psychological laws were known, we would still need to understand the concrete individual and the total situation in which the
individual exists before we could make any prediction about his
behaviour' (Chaplin and Krawice 1968:414), we nevertheless feel
that the perspectives put forward in this book, and the evidence to
support them, provide a useful and coherent framework from
which the psychological state of an unemployed person may be
viewed.

We define unemployment as a state of worklessness experienced by people who see themselves or are seen by others as potential members of the work force. This does not imply that people do not do anything when in this state, for by *work* we mean its modern usage relating to paid employment. As Williams points out, 'The specialization of (the meaning of) work to paid employment is the result of the development of capitalist productive relations' (Williams 1976:282). To be *in work* or *out of work* is to be in a definite relationship with some other who has control over the means of productive effort. The concept of work has partly shifted from the productive effort itself to the predominant social relationship. It is only in this sense that a woman running a house and bringing up children can be said to be not working. The unemployed, then, are those who are available for work but who are unable to secure work. It includes groups who have never been in employment, such as school leavers, and others who may have voluntarily terminated their employment but who now wish to re-enter the work force. In this sense the official figures for the number of unemployed people in the UK do not take into account numbers of people who are, in fact, unemployed. Many people, for example, married women, are available for and do want work, but are not included in the official figures because they see little point in registering as unemployed because they will not be entitled to welfare benefits.

Job loss we define as premature involuntary termination of employment. This definition excludes those who voluntarily retire or are involuntarily retired at the normal retirement age for their occupational group. While loss of work through retirement shares many common features with job loss through redundancy and dismissal, the individual's reaction to this transition appears to be different in character. Some of these differences are discussed briefly in Chapter 4.

We have not singled out unemployed school and college leavers as a special group, with the exception of brief discussions in Chapters 4 and 8. School and college leavers, like other people who are unemployed, have to adjust to a change and therefore engage in a process of transition. In their case the change may include the inability to secure a job they have desired and even been trained for, but never had. We feel that the basic model of transition presented in this book is applicable to their special circumstances. None the less, we believe that more research into this special transition is required.

The place work occupies in the life of women has dramatically changed over the years. These changes are not reflected in the many studies of unemployment reported in this book. In the majority of cases these studies examined only the effects of unemployment on men. Wherever possible we have included studies which have embraced women, and we believe that the models and explanations that we have developed are equally applicable to both men and women who have experienced unemployment.

Unemployment in the sense we use it in this book only occurs in those societies where productive effort is undertaken within work organizations by specialized groups of people. In primitive hunting and gathering societies work is all-pervasive. Mental and physical activity is primarily utilitarian in nature and it is impossible to draw any clear distinction between work and non-work. Consequently, it is unusual for people to be deprived of the opportunity to work because work is inextricably bound up with life. At times there may be little to do. People may be under-employed, may be idle, but they will not be unemployed in the sense that they are excluded from the work force. This contrasts sharply with the situation in industrial societies where people are employed in specialized capacities and where work, at least for the majority, is defined in such a way as to be a distinct and separate part of life. Under these conditions people can, and are, deprived of the opportunity to work.

Unemployment is unwelcome because of the special role and meaning work has in industrial society. This can be traced back to the teaching of Calvin. Calvin thought it proper for men to seek to progress through the occupational hierarchy. It was one's duty to extract the greatest possible gain from work, not to enjoy the fruits of labour, but to re-invest and create yet more work as a means towards establishing the Kingdom of God on earth. According to Tilgher (1930) it was this paradox, the command to ceaseless effort and to ceaseless renunciation of the fruits of effort, that laid the foundations of Puritanism. It also laid the foundation for an industrial labour force. Calvin preached that work must not be casual or occasional, but must be methodical, disciplined, rational, and uniform. His teachings also encouraged men to seek that work at which they were best, thus stimulating the development of a fluid labour force.

Max Weber in *The Protestant Ethic and the Spirit of Capitalism*

(1930), argued that it was the work ideologies fostered by the growth of the various religious sects, especially Calvinism, following the Reformation that gave rise to industrial capitalism. Although this view has been challenged, and while there may be some doubt as to the nature of the link between protestantism and capitalism, there is no doubt in the relationship between protestantism and the importance attributed to work. The protestant ethic lives on, in secularized form, in so far as the prevalent cultural norms attribute status and dignity to the worker, who is seen as a fully fledged and contributing member of society, and denies these same things to the non-worker.

Williams notes that whilst the modern meaning of unemployment depends upon its separation from the associations of *idle* ('it describes a social situation rather than a personal condition (idleness)'), there has been a steady ideological resistance to this necessary distinction. He argues that this resistance is still active and is evidenced by the frequent use of the word 'idle' in news reporting to describe workers laid off, locked out or on strike. 'With its strong moral implications idle in this context must have ideological intentions or effects. "Many thousands idle" sticks in the mind' (Williams 1976:275). Shimmin (1966) also points to the lingering Puritan tradition of work as a 'moral as well as a productive force', which shows itself in the overt and hidden fear associated with increased leisure.

Children, throughout their early socialization, are taught about the importance of work and learn that one of the prime sources of identity and status is one's occupation. Further, they learn that occupational advancement is synonymous with social advancement.

Sofer (1970), in his study of managers in mid-career, found that occupational or organizational 'rank' had important implications for prestige in the occupational community, the quality of relations with colleagues and their families, and for the way the individual evaluated his own prestige in relation to that of selected others. He also found that many managers in his study identified closely with what they did in the organization. He hypothesized that the origins of these identifications lay largely in the efforts made by senior managers to convince employees of the importance of what they were asked to do and in the need of the employees to find and establish themselves. Having found these opportunities and made corresponding commitments to him or herself and others, Sofer argued that the individual was disposed to build on and defend them. To be promoted was to receive confirmation that one has been building one's specializations in the right direction, and one's investment in one's particular occupational identity had been worthwhile. Sofer felt that, for the people in his study, promotion constituted the continued realization of their 'intended trend in life'. It gave meaning, purpose and continuity to what had been experienced in the past, was being experienced in the present and was to be experienced in the future. To be deprived of desired advancement can have important implications for felt identity. To be deprived of the opportunity to work can undermine the very foundations upon which the identity has been built.

SOCIAL ATTITUDES TOWARDS UNEMPLOYMENT

At the time of writing, in late 1980, when unemployment throughout the western world shows few signs of deviating from its recent rapid acceleration, there are indications that attitudes are slowly beginning to become more sympathetic and supportive towards the unemployed. Whilst we are not aware of any social surveys which have produced evidence to support such an assertion, our feelings and intuitions, which have developed in the process of interviewing a wide cross-section of people, would suggest that there has been some shift from viewing the unemployed as products of their own inadequacies to viewing unemployment as a product of the malfunctioning of an economic system.

This change is reflected in the media. Indeed, the media may have played a significant role in the change in public attitudes. In the mid- to late 1970s the media tended to concentrate on cases of abuse of the welfare system, and cases of what were presented as 'idle' and 'workshy' unemployed people (see Nutman 1977; Golding and Middleton 1978; Lythgoe 1979). This contrasts with the coverage in 1980 which has tended to concentrate on examining the economic causes and consequences of unemployment whilst at the same time giving attention to the hardship and suffering that many of the unemployed are having to endure. Thus the media are showing more concern with the plight of those bereft of work, and their predicament is being reported in terms which portray this concern rather than in terms of criticism and censure. Less blame for their worklessness is being laid at the feet of the unemployed.

None the less, there are still many people who find it difficult to dissociate unemployment from idleness. The dominance of the work ethic is such that many of the unemployed still perceive others as viewing them within a framework characterized by such terms and phrases as 'lazy', 'workshy', and 'living off the taxes that others have to pay'.

Even though an unemployed person is now able to view his or her predicament as being similar to that of millions of other people, the tendency we have found in our interviews and examination of the case studies of other researchers, is for the unemployed person to perceive his or her situation as a *particular* reflection on themselves. Whilst there are important arguments that suggest that this perception is culturally determined and that it may change if there is an adjustment away from the 'protestant work ethic', this adjustment, if it takes place, will inevitably be slow (and possibly painful). In this book we deal with the world of employment as it is, not as it ought to be, although in Chapter 9 we do give consideration to some of the possible avenues of change. As Orwell expressed it, even if the individual is part of a large group of unemployed people, for a person brought up in a work-oriented society, 'so long as Bert Jones across the street is still at work, Alf Smith is bound to feel himself dishonoured and a failure' (Orwell 1975:77).

In terms of help for the unemployed, we point out in Chapters 8 and 9 that most measures have focused on helping the individual to secure re-employment and this emphasis is being maintained, even though there is little prospect, in the foreseeable future, of securing employment for the millions unemployed.

Many older people, that is those over forty, who are unemployed today may never work again. It is possible that many of those who are currently leaving school may never work at all. Society is not yet ready to accept this possibility. By pursuing policies designed to re-establish the individual in work, society is effectively deciding that it is not necessary to develop and pursue policies designed to help the individual adjust to and cope with a state of sustained worklessness. Indeed, one consequence of an economic recession which results in high levels of unemployment, is the cut-backs and reductions in the subsidies to such areas as leisure pursuits and adult extra-mural education. Such activities could well form part of a coping strategy for individuals in dealing with the increased time they have because of their unemployment. Such a strategy is less likely to come into play because of the reduced availability or the increased cost of these activities.

The authors of this book are products of this work-oriented society. We both find it hard to conceive of our lives without work and we both share hopes that our children will be able to successfully develop work careers of their own. We find it difficult to come to terms with the possibility that they may never work, and we have done little or nothing to prepare them for this possibility, largely, we suspect, because we do not really know what to do. Society is faced with precisely the same dilemma. To do nothing, to refuse to admit that there is a need to plan for the possibility of an eventual workless majority, is not an appropriate response. Widespread worklessness, like the third world war, may never happen, but some contingency planning is called for none the less. This book does not undertake this monumental task. We recognize the need, and in due course, we hope to be able to make some contribution, but in the meantime we have chosen to focus our attention on the pursuit of a better understanding of the effects of worklessness on the individual within the current context of a society where people expect, and are expected, to work.

We have attempted to draw together the contributions of the many people who have been concerned with the psychological effects of unemployment. In addition we have included our own observations based on more than forty interviews with unemployed people. We are not totally satisfied with the outcome of this search for a theoretical model but we hope that the ideas we have attempted to weave into a consistent pattern may help some of those who decide to tread a similar path. The main contribution of our own conversations with unemployed people has been to illustrate the difficulties associated with attempting to develop a simple model to cover all cases, and they have pointed to the need to consider a variety of mediating factors which may explain behaviour which deviates from the norm. None the less we have been interested to note that the general model presented in Chapters 2 and 3 appears to apply to the vast majority who experience unemployment.

In the next chapter we describe the various stages which occur in the process of adjustment. Having put forward a basic model of transition in Chapter 2, in Chapter 3 we advance explanations for the process of adjustment in terms of a variety of psychological and social-psychological theories. Chapter 4 looks at differing reactions to unemployment and puts forward explanations of these in terms of the different forces which affect, and the differing meanings that work has for, various sub-groups of the unemployed. Chapters 5, 6, and 7 concentrate on particular aspects of the effects of unemployment. The possible health consequences are examined first, with consideration being given to the possible changes in both physical and mental health which may occur because of the individual's reaction to the loss of work. We then consider in Chapter 6 more specific evidence of the way in which the enforced position of unemployment affects the view a person has of himself or herself and how this view is 'managed' in interactions with other people. In Chapter 7 we consider the role of the job search and examine the differing functions that the activity of looking for a job may serve.

Finally, in Chapters 8 and 9 we examine strategies for helping the unemployed. Chapter 8 considers strategies to change the individual, and this has normally implied changing the individual so as to enhance his or her chances of regaining employment, whilst Chapter 9 briefly examines strategies to change the employing organizations in ways that make it easier for people to be reabsorbed into the labour force. We also consider in Chapter 9 strategies to change society in ways that will increase the demand for labour or in ways that will lead to the unemployed being accepted as full, if different, members of society.

2   Job loss as a psycho-social transition

> 'Unemployment is a form of crippling which can be expected to have the same effect as other forms of loss and it may be that society should become as sensitive to the damage inflicted on others by psychological mutilation as it is of the effects of physical mutilation.'
>
> PARKES 1971

In 1971 Colin Murray Parkes published what we feel to be an important paper outlining psycho-social transitions as a field for study. Parkes sees 'psycho-social transitions' as 'those major changes in life space which are lasting in their effects, which take place over a relatively short period of time and which affect large areas of the assumptive world' (Parkes 1971 : 103). 'Life space' is that part of the world with which the self interacts and in relation to which a person acts, and the 'assumptive world' is the totality of perceptions and conceptions that an individual holds about the world. In a sense, then, the two concepts of life space and assumptive world are dynamically interrelated, in that changes in the way we view the world will affect the significances of a variety of areas in our life space, and at the same time changes in our life space can affect the assumptions we make concerning our existence. In describing job loss as an example of a psycho-social transition Parkes brings out the nature of this relationship.

'Loss of job deprives a man of a place of work, the company of workmates and a source of income. It, therefore, produces several changes in his life space. What corresponding changes can be expected in the assumptive world? Clearly assumptions about the sources of money and security will change and the individual's faith in his own capacity to work effectively and to earn are also likely to change. His view of the world as a safe secure place will change, his expecations of his future and that of his family will change, and he is likely to have to replan his mode of life, sell possessions and maybe even move to a place where his prospects are better. Thus his altered assumptive world will cause him to introduce further changes in his life space, to set up a cycle of internal and external changes aimed at improving the "fit" between himself and his environment. In order properly to understand the effects of loss of job it is necessary to identify those areas of life space and the assumptive world which will or should change as a consequence of the initial changes in life space.'　　　　(Parkes 1971:103–04)

In a sense, the whole of this book is an attempt to delineate the changes in the life space and assumptive worlds that are a consequence of unemployment, and thus the framework put forward by Parkes should be seen as a major influence and guiding conceptual schema within which our thinking has been elaborated.

Bearing this in mind this chapter outlines some recent frameworks which have been put forward to describe the various phases and stages which individuals go through after becoming unemployed. All the writers we shall look at agree, either explicitly or implicitly, that the frameworks they are putting forward are essentially tentative and general but that they are nevertheless attempts at providing some basis from which a more detailed understanding of an individual's behaviour and psychological state may emerge. Thus Hopson and Adams state:

'We want to make it clear that seldom, if ever, does a person move from phase to phase. . . . It is rather more likely that these representations are of general experience and that any given individual's progressions and regressions are unique to his or her own circumstances.'

(Hopson and Adams 1976:13)

And Harrison, in a similar vein, states:

'It is crucial to remember that it is individuals – with their own distinctive personalities, expectations, and networks of relationships–who become unemployed. Their reactions both to the fact, and to the ensuing process, will obviously vary.'

(Harrison 1976:340)

The first framework examined is that put forward by Hopson and Adams (1976) which describes what they see as seven phases a person will go through in reacting to a psycho-social transition. The cycle of reactions and feelings which they describe is based on an analysis of the experiences of over 100 people who had attended transition workshops. Although these people were concerned with a variety of differing transitions we have supplemented the analysis by giving examples of the statements which unemployed people made to us during interviews.

The first stage of the transitional cycle is that of *immobilization*, where the person is overwhelmed by the event and is unable to reason, plan or understand what is happening. They are in a state of shock which is experienced as a feeling of numbness towards reality. A fifty-year-old man who had been unemployed for six weeks told us: 'When the boss came and told me I was finished it really took my breath away. I thought, "This can't be happening to me."'

The second stage is characterized by a *minimization* of the change, which involves attempts to maintain reality as if the event had not occurred. A fifty-five-year-old man who had been unemployed for six months said: 'I thought, great, it'll give me time to fix the garden properly.'

Eventually, Hopson and Adams argue, most people when confronted with evidence of a changed reality, come to realize that some changes in their way of living will have to be made. At this stage they become *depressed* because they are only beginning to face the fact that changes will have to be made, whilst at the same time not wanting nor knowing how to make these changes. This feeling is represented by a thirty-year-old woman who had been unemployed for two months when she said: 'You get depressed, and start to feel useless, and I think other people think I'm lazy.'

Eventually people start to realize that they have to *accept a changed reality*, and begin to release themselves from the assumptions of their pre-transitional situation. In moving on from this acceptance phase people now start to *test* out their new life space. In trying out new behaviours and attitudes they attempt to develop new ways of coping with their present reality. A thirty-three-year-old woman who had been unemployed for three months, told us how she went 'to Leeds or Bradford once a week – just to have a look round – for something to do – it gets me out of the house.' At this stage, however, there is a tendency for this testing to be within a framework of stereotypes, narrow classifications, and categories as to how things should or should not be. This activity of trying to establish a narrow conceptual framework develops into an attempt to realize a more comprehensive and meaningful frame of reference within which to understand and make sense of one's present situation.

If the individual is successful in his or her *search for meaning* and in his or her attempts to establish a viable conceptual framework, then this will be *internalized* as the new basis of that part of the assumptive world which has been affected by the transition. For example: a fifty-three-year-old man who had been unemployed for eighteen months said, 'I'd rather be behind a shop counter than at home, it's not my nature, but I can't do anything until my mother dies. You see, I'm the only one who can look after her.'

As stated, these seven phases (represented by the italic words or phrases), are based on an analysis of the case studies of over 100 people who had experienced some form of psycho-social transition. The relationship between an individual's self-esteem and the various phases is represented by Hopson and Adams in *Figure 2(1)*.

This relationship is drawn from accounts of a variety of different types of transition, and thus its contribution to our understanding of job loss must be seen in terms of providing a tentative framework from which an analysis of this particular transition might start. It must also be noted that this relationship has not been rigorously tested, although support for the view that unemployment is associated with an erosion of self-esteem is presented in Chapter 8. Hopson and Adams recognize the limitations of their schema and note that it 'is not systematic enough to be called a model, and not ambitious enough to be called a theory' (Hopson and Adams 1976:5).

A more specific framework describing the experience that the unemployed are likely to go through is given by Harrison (1976), in a paper reviewing the recent research on the psychological effects of long-term unemployment. Harrison argues that recent studies, especially in relation to those aged twenty-five to forty-five, who have had a past history of steady employment, tend to support the findings put forward by Eisenberg and Lazarsfeld (1938). In their summary paper of the evidence from research

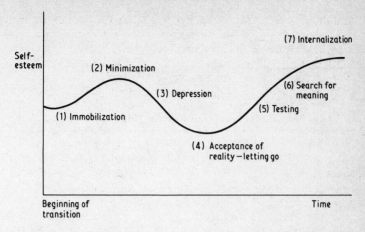

Figure 2(1)   Relationship between self-esteem and phases of the transitional cycle

Source: Hopson and Adams 1976:13.

carried out during the depression of the 1930s, Eisenberg and Lazarsfeld stated that:

> 'We find that all the writers who have described the course of unemployment seem to agree on the following points: First there is a shock, which is followed by an active hunt for a job, during which the individual is still optimistic and unresigned; he still maintains an unbroken attitude. Second, when all efforts fail, the individual becomes pessimistic, anxious, and suffers active distress; this is the most crucial state of all. And, third, the individual becomes fatalistic and adapts himself to his new state but with a narrower scope. He now has a broken attitude.'   (Eisenberg and Lazarsfeld 1938:378)

On the basis of Harrison's review of the evidence put forward in five recent studies, Sinfield (1970); Jones (1972); Herron (1975); Gould and Kenyon (1972); Marsden and Duff (1975), Harrison postulates a transitional cycle which involves the sequence of experiences of shock → optimism → pessimism → fatalism. His representation of this cycle (*Figure 2(2)*) bears close similarities to that put forward by Hopson and Adams (cf. *Figure*

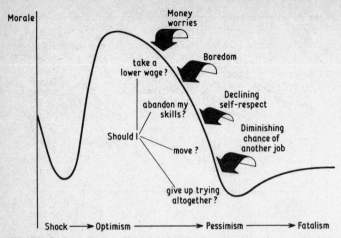

Figure 2(2)   The experience of unemployment

Source: Harrison 1976:339 (reproduced with the permission of the Controller of Her Majesty's Stationery Office).

2(1)). Both these graphical representations show an upturn towards the end of the cycle. Hopson and Adams show higher self-esteem when the individual has finally come to terms with his or her new status and Harrison shows some drop in morale. Whilst our encounters with the long-term unemployed and our reading of the literature suggest that in the long term adjustment tends to be associated with an acceptance of the situation and a movement away from disabling depressive states, their morale and self-esteem still appears to be substantially lower than that of the employed.

A more recent study and framework for describing the responses of people to unemployment has been put forward by Hill (1977; 1978). On the basis of a study of unemployed people in London and Merseyside in late 1976/early 1977, Hill postulates three discernible phases which he also claims are strikingly similar to those put forward by Eisenberg and Lazarsfeld in 1938. In the first phase, which Hill calls the *initial response*, the reaction can be traumatic. For example: A forty-six-year-old plasterer said, 'It's like someone cutting your throat', and a restaurateur recalled that he felt 'immediately degraded' and thought, 'I've become a statistic, I'm unemployed' (Hill 1978 : 118).

However, Hill found that more often than not the unemployed tended to deny that anything had really happened, and reacted with a level of optimism to their newly found freedom. For example: the restaurateur reported that for the first few days he thought, 'That's great, I can lie in in the morning, get up, sit down, go and wash the car and go for a little walk' (Hill 1978 : 118).

In the second phase, the *intermediate phase*, the individuals start the process of accepting the identity commensurate with their new life space, but as time proceeds they 'develop a kind of inertia that is psychologically debilitating. They feel insufficiently stimulated and undervalued.' They describe their condition in terms of depression, boredom, laziness. A thirty-year-old man out of work for ten months was asked what he did with his time: 'What can you do? I just stagnate' (Hill 1978 : 119). Awareness of this effect on some of the people studied resulted in attempts to fight against it, particularly in the early stages of this phase, but in general most moved on to the third phase, *settling down to unemployment*. In this stage the individual comes to adjust to his new life space. For example: a twenty-five-year-old single man who had been out of work for three years said, 'I've got adapted, but I didn't want to adapt. You could easily stay like that. I could be on the dole for the rest of my life' (Hill 1978 : 119). Also in this stage the anxiety, struggle and hope which were characteristics of the second phase, start to diminish as the individual becomes increasingly tolerant of, and adjusted to, the stability and routinization of his or her unemployed existence. In some cases even the depression associated with the second phase started to lift.

Finally, Katherine Briar's (1977) examination of the effects of long-term unemployment on workers and their families gives additional support to the notion of a transitional cycle associated with job loss. She describes similar reactions to those put forward in the preceding studies, but when describing the initial response she gives interesting illustrations of the manner in which people were informed of their impending unemployment. It seems that regardless of how they were told, it still felt like a 'shocking blow'. However, the lack of sensitivity to the workers' feelings which was often associated with the telling could only have heightened this shock. Two cases from the study illustrate this insensitivity:

'Jon, 63 years of age, has spent his entire working career in the ship building business. He was earning $12,000 and had worked his way up to the position of engineering manager. He had invested in his career, and had even attained a college education. After all his years of work, he was to learn of his job loss through a letter sent to him from his supervisor. The news shocked him and he felt like he'd been "kicked in the stomach".' (Briar 1977:44)

'Don was a 64 year old school counsellor. This college educated person had devoted his working career to acquiring the credentials to insure his working as a teacher or a counsellor. One day, while he was interviewing a student in his office he overheard the principal "yell the news around the corner". This news "flabbergasted him".' (Briar 1977:45)

Briar notes that the initial shock was followed by feelings of optimism about one's ability to find work, despite the prevailing high levels of unemployment in the area. The feelings of optimism and in some cases the expectations of acquiring higher salaries than those of their previous jobs, eventually waned, and the workers moved on to what Briar calls the second phase of unemployment, *joblessness as a way of life*. Characteristic of this phase is the shifting of blame for the individual's predicament from the system to the self, and also, as in the preceding studies, the onset of depression. One worker who had subsequently been re-employed recalled how 'he had become so depressed that he drew the curtains shut and sat in front of the TV staring at it all day, day after day' (Briar 1977:81). Others talked about the feeling of 'inertia' and 'nearly' giving up.

It would seem, in considering the various accounts given in this chapter, that there is a great deal of similarity both in the nature of the cycles put forward and in the categories and concepts used to describe the phases in these cycles (see *Table 2(1)*).

We conclude this chapter with a case study from Peter Townsend's (1979) extensive study of poverty in the UK. This case poignantly represents some of the feelings associated with the various stages in the transitional cycle produced by job loss.

'Mr Bradshaw was a bachelor of 60 who had been unemployed for thirty-four of the previous fifty-two weeks when first

Table 2(1) *Self-esteem changes during transitions*

	immobilization	minimization	depression	test accept reality	search for meaning	internalization
Hopson and Adams (1976)	immobilization	minimization	depression	test accept reality	search for meaning	internalization
Harrison (1976) (Eisenberg and Lazarsfeld (1938))	shock	optimism	pessimism		fatalism	
Hill (1977)	initial response (trauma, denial)		intermediate phase (depression, accept reality)		settling down to unemployment (adaptation)	
Briar (1977)	job loss (shock, optimism)		joblessness as a way of life (self blame, depression)		inertia	

interviewed in May 1968. He lived in a two-roomed flat in Nottingham and was on the Disabled Persons' Register. Four years earlier, as a lorry driver for British Rail, he had had a coronary and was partially paralysed on his left side. He was then forced to take a succession of light temporary jobs and had been last in a routine clerical job in the Town Hall.

In the summer of 1968, he obtained work as a weighbridge clerk with a scrap merchant, and held this job for two years. . . . He then became unemployed for most of the next two years (having one clerical job at the time of the 1971 Census for ten weeks). For many months he had tried hard to get work:

"I was offered 15p an hour as a watchman from 7 p.m. to 7 a.m., seven days a week. It was like going to prison for seven nights a week. I can't use the language to you I used to them. I used to tramp all around town looking for work – writing (they never bothered to answer, never got any replies, waste of postage). It takes all the guts out of you. You're on the scrap heap now if you're over 30. They don't want to know. They make excuses about the superannuation scheme. The last job I had I saw in the news. I rang up right away. They told me my age was against me but that Saturday morning there was a knock at the door, and there was the Manager. He said, 'Can you start on Monday?' What a lift that was, I can tell you. I thought, 'I'm made for life now.' Then came this takeover and that was that. I must have applied for over 1000 jobs."

He gets (1972) £8.20 supplementary benefit (which includes an allowance for a diabetes diet). He has been obliged to return his T.V. set to a rental firm because he could not afford the rental of 50p per week. "I scratch along. I just make it. I can't afford cinemas or anything like that. This enforced idleness has been a bit of a let down, I can tell you. Somehow I've got so that I accept it, but it's not living. It's no joke to know you're no use. It doesn't seem right that all your time is spent just keeping yourself alive. . . . Somebody said the poor are always with us. Was it Jesus Christ? It might have been Ted Heath. I don't know. Big money rules the world, not Christianity or charity. It always has and it always will.''

(Townsend 1979:607)

It appears that the transition can be viewed in terms of three broad stages. Within the first of these is an initial phase of shock

and immobilization, followed by a phase characterized by re-
newed hope, optimism and a tendency to minimize or deny that
there has been a change. The second broad stage seems to include
a period in which the idea that 'things will turn out all right in the
end' is shaken and the individual's identity comes under pressure.
This stage often appears to be associated with depression and
withdrawal. The onset of this stage is characterized by an acceptance that there has been a change and by a 'letting go' of the past,
and during this second stage the individual gradually begins to
search for and test out new relationships between self and
situation. If unemployment is prolonged and if re-call to the lost
job fails to materialize then the individual must find and in-
ternalize a new identity. This process of readjustment is characterized in the third and final broad stage irrespective of whether
the individual successfully re-enters the world of work in a new
work role or continues in a state of unemployment. Bakke (1960)
notes that an important prerequisite of readjustment is acceptance of the fact that achievements of the past can no longer be
made standards for the satisfaction of achievements in the
present. It is as though the period of disorganization and crisis
unfreezes both the individual and his or her family and helps
them to search for and find new values and standards better suited
to the present.

3 Psychological perspectives on the transitional cycle of unemployment

'The person who has been told he is no longer wanted at work feels useless. The ensuing depression results in his getting at odds with everyone, his wife and family and friends, or he becomes insular, cutting himself off from everyone and everything.'

Consultant Psychiatrist

In this chapter we briefly present Lewin's (1935) 'field-force' theory as a backcloth against which we can examine the contribution of other psychological theories to our understanding of the individual in transition. From the perspective of field theory, the unemployed individual's initial response can be viewed in terms of an attempt to maintain forces which sustain his or her previous state of equilibrium. As the period of unemployment extends the individual's changing reaction may be viewed in terms of Vroom's (1964) expectancy theory and the theory of cognitive dissonance advanced by Festinger (1957). The work of Ellis (1973a; 1973b) may help our understanding of the depression and pessimism associated with the later phases in the transition. Finally, Seligman's (1975) theory of 'helplessness' may provide an explanation of the differing depths of the depression which affects individuals.

We see the psychological perspectives advanced in this chapter as possible ways of explaining the various phases through which an individual tends to pass when unemployed. We offer these explanations as conceivable frameworks within which individual cases may be analysed. To this end, then, we are not saying this *is* what will happen but rather that here is a way of looking at what may happen to an unemployed person.

The main reason for adopting this tentative approach is that the consequences of unemployment 'are far from obvious and are highly variable depending on the dispositions of the individuals who have become unemployed and on the duration of their unemployment, and on the social and cultural context in which the unemployed are embedded.'

(Hyman 1979:282)

Coupled with this is the argument of Lewin put forward in the previous chapter that

'even if all psychological laws were known, we would still need to understand the concrete individual and the total situation in which the individual exists before we could make any predictions about his behaviour.'

(Chapline and Krawice 1968:414)

Kurt Lewin (1935) proposed a model of change in which he viewed behaviour as a result of a dynamic balance of forces working in opposite directions. He argued that change occurs when these forces get out of equilibrium and a process of unfreezing takes place. Based on homeostatic assumptions a process of change occurs (moving), as the individual attempts to bring the forces back into equilibrium. These attempts, if successful, result in the consolidation of a new position of equilibrium (refreezing). Whilst it is the totality of forces at work in any particular case which determines behaviour, we shall on occasion be looking at particular forces in the field, remembering Lewin's argument that no unequivocal relation obtains between the magnitude of the forces and the amount of energy in the process. On the contrary, relatively slight forces may, when the whole field is appropriately formed, control relatively large amounts of energy. This model of an individual at the centre of a 'force-field' (akin to the concept in physics) is presented here in order to provide a theoretical backcloth against which other psychological theories and explanations may be viewed.

Following Lewin, then, it might be argued that any change in the forces acting upon an individual which are perceived by him or her as a threat to the self-concept will tend to be resisted. The individual will strive to resist such changes in an attempt to maintain the old equilibrium. What support is there for this hypothesis in the context of the individual's initial reaction to unemployment?

MINIMIZATION

Both Hill (1977) and Briar (1977) found that some of the people they researched actually took a holiday soon after they became unemployed, and, whilst one interpretation of this may be in terms of the availability of opportunity, we would suggest that this behaviour is also explicable in terms of someone attempting to maintain a life space consistent with a self-image of an employed person. A holiday being an activity that many employed people engage in at some time of the year, is a readily available and concrete reaffirmation of an unchanged life space. It may also be seen as a means of escape.

Another form of behaviour that Hill found, especially among those without family responsibilities, was that some people delayed claiming welfare benefits. Again, an interpretation of this may be made in terms of lack of knowledge in the early stages of the availability of benefits, but the fact that it is those without family responsibilities and therefore perhaps fewer financial worries who are more likely to delay claiming, would suggest that the delay in claiming benefit is more an attempt to deny the need to change. One of the facets of unemployment which several people whom we interviewed who had recently lost their jobs pointed out as being an unpleasant factor of unemployment, was 'signing on' (i.e. registering for unemployment benefit). Similar findings are also reported by other researchers and journalists. For example, an unemployed man interviewed on a Thames Television programme (*TV Eye* 5 June 1980), said, 'I resent the fact that I had to sign on the dole, or become in me own opinion, a second class citizen.' It might be hypothesized that the delay in 'signing on' serves a number of functions. For example, it may enable the individual to avoid a series of experiences which would require an alteration in his or her assumptive world. It may also help maintain the belief that the present situation is temporary.

Another reaction, though reported less frequently, is that some people actually go on a spending spree. Depending on the reason for unemployment, money, in the early stages, tends not to be short. (People may receive money in lieu of notice, may have worked a week or fortnight in hand, receive holiday pay or tax rebates, and the like.) Spending more than usual may be interpreted as irresponsible, but within the framework put forward here, it may be seen as an attempt by the individual to demonstrate that they don't need to worry about the future and their present situation is merely a temporary well-financed break in employment.

Finally, for some of the unemployed reported in Briar's (1977) and Townsend's (1979) studies, the desire to retain old relationships between themselves and their life spaces was such that they were prepared to wait for recall to their original jobs. As Townsend put it, 'Some were so determined to seek re-engagement at their last place of employment that they were, at first, unwilling to contemplate anything else' (Townsend 1979:611). It seems, therefore, in considering some of the initial reactions to unemployment, that many people not only perceive their situation as unchanged ('The first few days you sit at home and relax, it's like a holiday'), but actually strive to create the conditions under which this idiosyncratic perception can be maintained.

OPTIMISM TO PESSIMISM

After the 'holiday' is over the individual has to begin to organize his or her daily activity and commence the process of looking for work. As the Pilgrim Trust study in the 1930s pointed out,

'Work provides for most people the pattern within which their lives are lived, and when this pattern is lost they have thrown upon them the responsibility which, in the case of most unemployed men, their working lives in no way qualified them to bear, the responsibility for organizing their own existence.'
(Pilgrim Trust 1968:149)

At this stage, however, their belief in the transience of the situation and expectation of future employment are still powerful forces for some people, and many are able to develop some routine of daily life. One man we interviewed said that for the first month he was fully occupied in applying for jobs, going for interviews, and redecorating the house. The extent to which gardening, decorating and do-it-yourself activities are frequently mentioned by the unemployed as ways of filling in the days, especially in the early stages of unemployment, is another sign of the individual's striving to maintain an image of himself or herself as a 'worker'. One man interviewed by Marsden and Duff (1975) referred to his activity in his potting shed as 'my work'.

In response to employment-seeking activities the individual

may begin to receive rejections from job interviews and applications, and, in terms of the transitional cycle discussed in Chapter 2, may start to move from the initial response to the intermediate phase (Hill); from the minimization to depression phase (Hopson and Adams); and from the optimism to pessimism stages (Harrison). Can we give an account of the psychological change that is occurring at this stage in the transition?

It seems that at this stage two of the driving forces motivating the individual to seek work, which at the same time are equilibrium maintaining forces in relation to self-image, are the beliefs that work is available and can be obtained. Changes in these beliefs, with the concomitant changes in an individual's assumptive world can be explained in terms of an expectancy model, which had its origins in the work of Lewin (1938) and Tolman (1932). The formulation put forward by Vroom (1964) is that an individual's behaviour is a function of three factors.

(1) The perceived instrumentality of an action for reaching a goal, this being the perception that particular actions are necessary for achieving a certain goal.
(2) The value or valence of the goal to the individual, that is, the desirability or otherwise of the outcome to the individual.
(3) The expectation that an act will lead to a given outcome. This differs from instrumentality in that it refers to the individual's belief that were he or she to behave in the particular manner required to achieve their desired goal, then this would actually result in the achievement of this goal.

Applying this theory to the present situation we have the individual perceiving that applying for a job is an essential action towards getting employment (instrumentality), that getting employment is a highly valued goal (valence), and finally, the belief that applying for a job will lead to employment (expectancy). The outcome – securing employment – is a first-level outcome which may be instrumental in leading to second-level outcomes with higher valences (i.e. it may be that getting work is not valued highly *per se*, but only in so far as it is a means of getting money, self-esteem, etc.) In relation to this point Marie Jahoda (1979) spells out possible outcomes when she differentiates between the latent and manifest functions that are implicit in the psychological meaning of work. The manifest functions are the pay and conditions, but it is through an understanding of the latent functions such as the structuring of time, the sense of purpose, the opportunity for achievement and the like, that she believes we can see why work is psychologically supportive and goes beyond simply the need to earn money. These functions are discussed more fully in Chapter 4.

What then happens when the individual performs in the way that is predicted by the expectancy theory, but finds that his or her expectations are incorrect (i.e. applying for jobs does not lead to employment)? It would seem that the initial rejections with all the 'information' they generate appear to have little effect either on the expectations or the desirability of the outcome. One of the people we interviewed, who had been unemployed for six weeks and had been turned down for five jobs said, 'It's early days yet. I didn't expect to walk straight into a new job.'

An explanation of this in terms of the maintenance of the 'equilibrium' of the self-concept is that to accept these rejections as significant comments about one's position will require an alteration of one's assumptions about that position. With continuing failure to secure employment, however, the feedback from rejections becomes more obvious and thus more difficult to ignore, both by the individual and those close to him or her. At this stage the individual moves from a state of attitudinal consonance in which his or her beliefs, feelings and dispositions to take action regarding employment are all positive, to a state in which, whilst the feelings and dispositions to take action might be positive, the beliefs about the future expectations of employment are becoming increasingly negative. In so far as this new state of cognitive dissonance is psychologically uncomfortable, the individual will try by a variety of means to return to a position of consonance (Festinger 1957). It is at this point that some of the unemployed struggle hardest to find employment. The increased intensity of the search for employment is often a desperate attempt to return to a position of employment in which the self-concept can be secured, but it is just this desperation of effort, which, if unsuccessful, can move an individual more rapidly into the next phase in the transitional cycle.

An analogy may help illustrate this point. Many people who have run races of, let us say, 5000 metres against opponents who are better than they are, know the feeling of having to try harder to keep up with the leaders. At a certain point, when they are starting to lose contact, they make a desperate effort to keep up and regain the leading group. Even if they are successful, it is only temporary, because the opposition continue to run at too fast a pace. The next time the field begins to move away, the runner is unable to stop them, as he or she has used up all energy and willpower at the first attempt to keep up with the leaders. This time he or she moves quickly back through the field. It is in this sense that the unemployed who make the burst and struggle harder to maintain the old relationship between themselves and their life space, if unsuccessful, move quickly into the phase of pessimism and depression.

For many, however, the process is a less abrupt move with the unfreezing from their original assumptions taking place gradually as more and more rejections accumulate. The reality of the rejections which confront the individual in the morning mail and in the post-interview 'I'm sorrys', can no longer be screened as they were in the early stages of unemployment. The individual has now to develop alternative assumptions and beliefs to account for the situation that he or she is coming to perceive as reality. The process of change in relation to the individual's expectations about employment involves a cognitive redefinition of him- or herself and the situation and the consequent development of new personal constructs. It is through this process that the individual starts to accept that he or she stands little or no chance of securing employment. As one person put it, 'Who's going to set me on?' In terms of the phases in the transitional cycle discussed in the previous chapter, the phase the individual is now at is perhaps the most multiplex in relation to the cognitions he or she holds about him- or herself and reality. To put this another way, the individual's assumptive world is now a network of dissonant ideas, beliefs, and behaviours. Thus, at the same time as accepting that he or she will not be able to get a job, the individual is also unable to conceive of life without one. The individual applies for jobs but is now conscious of the futility of such actions. This is expressed in a powerful way by a twenty-eight-year-old mechanic who had been unemployed for four months in the 1930s. 'It isn't the hard work of tramping about so much, although that's bad enough. It's the hopelessness of every step you take when you go in search of a job you know isn't there' (Bakke 1933). It is also expressed in the 1980s by a man who had worked for twenty years in what he believed was a secure job in the shipyards, 'You go to firms, you feel as if you're begging

like when you see people you know, and when it starts getting
you down, and then you start going up to the Job Centre, which
they do their best, but it's not much help' (Thames Television).
Another of the unemployed interviewed in the same programme
said, 'The realization's sunk in that there's just no jobs around.
The clerk told me that I had picked the wrong time of the year to
become unemployed.'

Whilst an individual's expectations about employment may be
becoming more realistic it is common at this stage for the psychological defences that are erected in order to make sense of this
predicament to come under attack from those closest to the
individual. The wife of one of the unemployed interviewed by
Marsden said:

> 'I suppose this last week or two I have begun to nag him a bit
> and get on at him to put a bit more time into finding a job.
> There must be some more papers he could get, with more jobs
> in that he could apply for. You see, I don't quite see things the
> same way as he does.'

Similarly a letter to an agony column states:

> 'Like so many men these days, I am unemployed and we've
> been going through a tricky spell because of the difficulties of
> finding a job. My wife nags me. Even my kids – aged seven and
> nine – don't seem to have much respect for me. . . . My wife
> says all our troubles are due to my lack of interest in work.
> This isn't true. I am not a layabout and would give anything to
> have a job I enjoy, if only I could find the right slot.'
>
> > (*Daily Mirror* 26 May 1980)

By this stage the individual will have completed most of the
'work' that 'needed' to be done in the house and garden, and this,
coupled with the now changed financial circumstances, means
that changes will have to be made in daily activities. 'It costs
money decorating, and you can't keep it up. Mostly it's just
pottering. I get bored stiff' (Marsden and Duff 1975 : 192). One
man we interviewed in a pub had been made redundant six weeks
previously. He said, 'I'll have to stop coming here. I've been
coming here early doors after work for a couple of pints for years
now. I can't see the wife letting me come now I'm not working.'

The point implicit in the above quotation is that at this stage it
is not simply a question of an individual altering only his or her

constructs about the availability of work, but rather that there are a whole cluster of areas of the assumptive world that are now being threatened by the changed position, all of which may require a cognitive re-evaluation. Perhaps for most individuals the changing perception of the availability of work is the major focus, but in the light of the above, analysing this aspect in isolation from the range of factors affecting the individual at this stage, would give an unreal view of what the individual is going through.

DEPRESSION

In terms of a psychological explanation of the effect of holding this multiplex and often dissonant assumptive world, the work of Albert Ellis (1973a; 1973b) may throw light on the depressive and pessimistic emotional existence that many unemployed inevitably come to.

Ellis's view is that when a highly charged emotional consequence (C – anxiety and depression), follows a significant activating event (A – becoming unemployed), then 'A' may appear to, but does not actually cause 'C'. Rather 'C' is created by 'B' the individual's belief system. The anxiety and depression of the unemployed, Ellis would argue, is caused not by the fact of unemployment *per se*, but is rather the consequence of the irrational beliefs that the individual adopts in relation to being unemployed. The assumptions within this perspective place the individual at the centre of his or her world as a person who behaves not only reactively in response to the environment, but proactively in that it is he or she who is developing and deciding in many cases what he or she believes (however incorrectly) is the optimum way of coping. As Adler puts it:

> 'No experience is a cause of success or failure. We do not suffer from the shock of our experiences – the so called trauma – but we make out of them just what suits our purpose. We are self determined by the meaning we give to our experiences; and there is probably something of a mistake involved when we take particular experiences as the basis of our future life.'
>
> (Quoted in Ellis 1973a:168)

In a sense many of the idiosyncratic reactions to unemployment are a result of the differences in the individual personalities, coupled with the Adlerian precept that

'The individual . . . does not relate himself to the outside world in a predetermined manner, as is often assumed. He relates himself always according to his own interpretation of himself and his present problems. . . . It is his attitude toward life which determines his relationship to the outside world.'

(Quoted in Ellis 1973a : 167)

Based on this perspective, Ellis postulates that humans are self-talking, self-evaluating beings, and that many of the emotional problems stem from the fact that they misleadingly or irrationally define their preferences as absolute needs. Ellis' approach may help to distinguish between the frustration, annoyance, and worry of the early stages of unemployment, and the depression and pessimism of the later phases. He says:

'The basic tenet of RET (Rational Emotive Therapy) is that emotional upsets, as distinguished from feelings of sorrow, regret, annoyance and frustration, are caused by the individual's irrational Beliefs and that these Beliefs are irrational because they magically insist that something in the universe should, ought, or must be different from the way it indubitably is.'

(Ellis 1973a : 178)

Ellis believes that there are a finite number of these irrational beliefs and that they can be reduced to the 'irrational trinity':

(1) Because it would be highly preferable if I were outstandingly competent, I absolutely should and must be; it is awful when I am not; and I am therefore a worthless individual.
(2) Because it is highly desirable that others treat me considerately and fairly, they absolutely should and must, and are rotten people who deserve to be utterly damned when they do not.
(3) Because it is preferable that I experience pleasure rather than pain, the world absolutely should arrange this and life is horrible, and I can't bear it when the world doesn't.

When we conducted some of our interviews we did not have Ellis' theory in mind, but on re-reading our notes it would appear to us that many of our interviewees were implicitly describing aspects of the 'irrational trinity'. It would seem, therefore, that an approach adopting Ellis' theory may throw light on the depression that people were experiencing. A forty-two-year-old woman, who had been unemployed for three months, and who said that she was feeling demoralized and depressed described her attitudes to getting work in the following way:

'If you're unlucky with a few interviews, you begin to feel that nobody wants you – you begin to think that other people think you are lazy. I think age comes into it, when you're over forty it's harder to get a job. Managers are damned unfair, you feel you can't win – they say they don't want girls, they don't want older people, it seems that what they want is a spinster in her mid-thirties.'

A forty-three-year-old man, who had been laid off five months previously, said: 'I've lost interest. Why bother going for a job when you know you won't get it? The longer you're off the worse it gets, it eats into you. I'm disillusioned with society – what sort of a country is it where a man cannot get work?' Later when discussing how he filled his time, 'I used to go to the club at night, but I've stopped going, even people I thought were alright started passing remarks about how they were keeping me. I just got fed up with them.'

It would appear that many of the unemployed at this stage are depressed and downhearted because they are still adopting unrealistic and irrational ideas about how their lives *should* be.

Eventually many of the unemployed start to settle down to being unemployed, and develop a routine and life-style commensurate with their new status and situation. Whilst for some the emotional anxiety and depression of the intermediate phase remains, though now with a more muted intensity, for others, their assumptive worlds are now based on a sullen and despondent acceptance of their life on the dole. Thus, coupling Lewin with Ellis, it would appear that the energy of the irrational ideological forces is waning.

One psychological explanation of this move in the transitional cycle is based on the assumption of Lewin that individuals need and will strive to attain some form of equilibrium in their assumptive worlds, and secondly, that when confronted with information which is perceived as 'real' but which cannot sustain previous assumptions that an individual held about him- or herself and the world, then these assumptions cannot be maintained and will eventually be reconstructed.

It is through this reconstruction of social reality that the individual comes to accept himself or herself and adapt to the situation as an unemployed person. As Jones argues the end of the cycle for some is a

'total change in personality. A man becomes institutionalised in unemployment as do men in prisons and hospitals. Consciously, he wants to get out; at a deeper level he doesn't. He has received too many rejections. He has come to accept that he is a failure, and at this deeper level, prefers not to be disturbed in that role. It is common, (employment) managers say, for such a man to be informed of a possible job, and told to present himself for interview, and to miss the appointment. This is the stage of final defeat, it is the ruin of a man.'

(Jones 1972 : 102)

Whilst the above describes a total change in an individual's assumptive world, the reduction in the desire to get a job, which in most cases comes gradually, can be given some explanation in terms of avoidance motivation (Cohen and Zimbardo 1962). One of the long-term unemployed interviewed by Marsden and Duff said he

'Stopped even looking for a job, really in the finish I did, really in them two years I lost all interest. I think at that time I became a bit of a hermit. I think if I had not been married, and no responsibilities at all, I think I'd have gone and walked out, probably just went on the road or something. I really believe I would have done it.'

(Marsden and Duff 1975 : 201)

This drop in the desire for finding a job manifests itself not only in the reduction of job-seeking activity, but also in the behaviour and dress people adopt when going for interviews. Several personnel managers have said they can spot someone who doesn't want work: 'For a start they don't seem bothered whether they get the job or not.' The findings of Cohen and Zimbardo (1962), which were subsequently supported by the derivative work of Schlachet (1962), make a relevant and important point in relation to job-securing activity. They found that although common sense might reason that a person who gets a lot of failures would try to improve his or her conditions in order to reduce the chances of failure, it turns out that the individual who feels he or she stands a moderate chance of gaining success, is the one most likely to take advantage of the opportunity to improve his or her conditions. Their explanation of this in terms of cognitive dissonance theory is that given a certain incentive, the greater the prospect of failure to which a person commits himself or herself, the more dissonance he or she should experience, and the more he or she should attempt to reduce that dissonance by a decrement in motivation. This would be reflected in less concern with changing the conditions so as to ensure a greater probability of success on future occasions. Thus the more the person is committed and convinced that he or she has no chance of securing employment, the less he or she will be concerned to create the conditions such that he or she will get employment.

FATALISM

Another explanation of the psychological changes that take place in the move from pessimism to fatalism, and which includes an explanation of the above, could be given in terms of a framework which involves the concepts of powerlessness, helplessness, and uncontrollability, at one extreme, and, autonomy, self-direction, and controllability at the other.

Tiffany, Cowan, and Tiffany (1970) adopted this perspective in their analysis of psychological problems as a cause of unemployment and quote Angyal (1965 : 12) as stating that, 'Disturbances of autonomous strivings form an important aspect of work inhibition, an ubiquitous condition of neurosis.' Whilst tending to examine the relationship as one in which psychological problems cause unemployment, they were nevertheless aware of the dynamic interactive nature of the causality. In discussing various studies using Rotter's (1954) internal-external control dimensions they argue, for example, that people who are more internally controlled, i.e. believe that outcomes are related to their behaviour, are more likely to see obstacles as surmountable and respond to stress adaptively. On the other hand 'as the locus of control becomes more external, frustration reactions become less constructive, debilitating anxiety reactions increase, and facilitative anxiety reactions decrease' (Tiffany, Cowan, and Tiffany 1970 : 78). This is another way of describing the reactions of many unemployed people as they start to perceive that their chances of securing employment are a function of forces outside their control. In the final analysis this despondent acceptance of the locus of control as being external to the individual means that he or she becomes unaware of the possibilities that may arise through which he or she could exert control and regain employment. As Seeman (1963) says, 'Man is sensitive to cues in his environment only when he believes he can have some effect upon it.'

A similar account of the psychological reactions in the later phases of unemployment could also be given in terms of Seligman's (1975) theory of 'Helplessness'. Seligman proposes a theory in which he claims that individuals, when exposed to uncontrollable events, learn that responding is futile. Such learning undermines the incentive to respond and so produces profound interferences with the motivation of instrumental behaviour. It also, he claims, interferes with learning that responding works, when events do actually become controllable, and thus it produces cognitive distortions. He further claims that if the event is important for the individual then he or she will feel anxious as long as he or she is uncertain of the uncontrollability of the outcome, and then the perception of certainty in relation to the uncontrollability of the outcome produces depression. Some of these findings could be explained in terms of the theories of Lewin, Vroom, and Festinger, that have already been mentioned, but Seligman goes further and examines the transferability of 'learned helplessness' in one situation to other situations in which the individual is involved.

In trying to explain the conditions under which expectations that events are uncontrollable will not be formed, even when the individual actually experiences uncontrollability, he postulates three factors: immunization by contrary expectancy; immunization by discriminative control; and relative strengths of outcomes. Immunization by contrary expectancy relates to previous situations which the individual has experienced. If the individual has had a history of experiences in which he or she has had control over outcomes, then this will be internalized, and he or she will have difficulty in learning that outcomes are uncontrollable. Thus, the individual will have greater difficulty in learning that expectations that job-seeking behaviour will lead to employment are actually unrealistic. The second factor, immunization by discriminative control, refers to the ability to differentiate situations in terms of their controllability. If the individual has learned in one situation that he or she has control, and he or she becomes helpless in another situation, then he or she will discriminate between the controllability of the two situations. The final factor, which might limit the transferability of learned helplessness, is the relative significance of the situation. This factor is important for understanding the behaviour of individuals when faced with uncontrollability in job-securing activity. What it states is that uncontrollability in situations perceived by the individual as trivial, will not be transferable to situations perceived by the individual to be important. However, uncontrollability in situations seen as important and significant by the individual *will be* transferable to other less important and trivial situations.

What follows from this is that the effects of uncontrollability in job-securing activity, on an individual's overall psychological state and on behaviour in other situations, will depend on the extent to which the 'occupational self-concept' is central to the personality. For individuals where work is central to their self-concept, one would predict that the effect of being unable to realize this part of their personality may be traumatic and may transfer to other facets of their personality and behaviour. For individuals whose occupational self-concept is less central or even peripheral, the effects will be less traumatic and less likely to transfer to other situations.

In applying Seligman's theory to the unemployed, the first factor – 'immunization by contrary expectancy' – can be elaborated. If an individual has had several minor experiences of unemployment and then re-employment, then according to Seligman it will take longer to learn that he or she is not going to get a job. Consequently, the individual will be less likely to suffer the emotional and psychological effects of helplessness.

'For myself, well, since I've left school I've been on and off. I've never really had a steady job, d'you know what I mean. I'm not a man who's been somewhere all my life and when the crunch comes worries, "Oh what am I going to do now?" I always know something will turn up. Something always does in our game.'   (Marsden and Duff 1975:191)

The other side of the coin of immunization by contrary expectancy is the case of the individual who has never failed, and who consequently has never had to cope with the anxiety and frustration that accompanies failure. Seligman's argument in this case is centred on the emotional development of the child and young adult, but the effects he describes seem to help to account for the different reactions of adults who have little or no experience of failure. Seligman says:

'If a young adult has no experience of coping with anxiety and frustration, if he never fails and then overcomes, he will not be able to cope with failure, boredom and frustration when it becomes crucial. Too much success, too coddled an existence, makes a child helpless when he is finally confronted with his first failure.' (Seligman 1975:157)

It is on the lines of the predisposing factors given above that a possible explanation can be given for the greater intensity of emotional reaction and psychological change that appears to affect the more ambitious and successful individuals when confronted with unemployment. It also seems that a similar perspective may help to illuminate the differential effects of unemployment on those who have been in the same job for years, compared to those who have changed jobs and perhaps experienced brief periods of frictional unemployment. We quote at length the following case study given by Seligman, because it includes not only a history of the case, but also a description of the psychological effects of job change and unemployment, which are commonly described in the research and which our own field work supports.

'Recently, a 42-year-old business executive, temporarily unemployed, came to see me for some vocational advice. Actually, it was his wife who first contacted me; having read a popular article of mine on helplessness, she asked me to talk with her husband, Mel, because he looked helpless to her. For the last twenty years Mel had been a rising executive; up until a year ago he had been in charge of production for a multi-million-dollar company involved in the space programme. When the government decreased its financial support for the space research, he lost his job, and was forced to take a new executive position in another city, in a company he described as "back-biting". After six miserable months he quit. For a month he sat listlessly around the house, and made no effort to find work; the slightest annoyance drove him into a rage of anger; he was unsocial and withdrawn. Finally, his wife prevailed on Mel to take some vocational guidance tests that might help him find a satisfying job.

When the results of these tests came back, they revealed that he had a low tolerance for frustration, that he was unsociable, that he was incapable of taking responsibility, and that routine, prescribed work best fit his personality. The vocational guidance company recommended that he became a worker on an assembly line. This advice came as a shock to Mel and his wife, since he had twenty years of high executive achievement behind him, was usually outgoing and persuasive, and was much brighter than most sewing machine operators. But these tests actually reflected his present state of mind: he believed every small obstacle insurmountable, he was not interested in other people, and he could barely force himself to get dressed, much less make important career decisions. But this profile did not give a true picture of Mel's character; rather it reflected a process, probably temporary, that had been going on since he lost his job – the disorder of depression.'

(Seligman 1975:75)

SUMMARY

In this chapter we have tried to follow the path of the transitional cycle described in the previous chapter, giving at each stage a psychological explanation or account, which we believe helps to understand in more detail the reasons for, and effects of, the various changes that occur during the transition.

In general we have tended to assume a dynamic model of personality in which understanding what is happening is seen not only in terms of the way in which external forces and changing circumstances impinge on a person, but more importantly in terms of the variety of ways in which individuals construe and react to these changes. Many forces in Lewin's model of individual behaviour may be influenced by external factors, but their number, type, and magnitude is a function of the meanings and strengths which are assigned to them by individuals. Given this dynamic model of personality our analysis has not assumed a particular self-image.

The essential point is that the similarity of the transitional experience is not necessarily a function of the similarity of the self-images of differing people, but rather a function of the similarity in the means by which individuals realize what may be quite diverse self-images. It is the loss of the means that gives rise to the psycho-social transition.

In the following chapter we shall explain what might be called 'mediating influences' in an attempt to account for some of the diversity of reaction to unemployment. These 'mediating influences' apply to certain individuals and groups of individuals and affect not only the length of the transitional cycle, but also the amplitude of the various phases. In terms of the structure of this exploration of the psychological effects of unemployment, we are moving from a general psychological account of the transitional cycle to an examination of the effects of particular facets or variables which may help to explain some of the different effects of unemployment on individuals.

4 The individual's attitude to work and unemployment

'I like work: it fascinates me. I can sit down and look at it for hours. I love to keep it by me: the idea of getting rid of it nearly breaks my heart.'

JEROME K. JEROME, *Three Men in a Boat*, 1889

In the previous chapter we advanced several psychological theories which we believe provide some explanation of the transitional cycle through which many unemployed people appear to progress. Generalized frameworks, of the kind advanced in Chapters 2 and 3, can provide indicators for the analysis of most cases, they can also be useful in providing a perspective from which to analyse why people may deviate from an apparently 'normal' pattern of adjustment. This chapter looks at what work and unemployment can mean for the individual and attempts to explain why everybody will not experience the transition from work to unemployment in the same way. After re-examining the functions that work can serve for the individual, which we briefly discussed in the previous chapter, we consider what working and not working may actually mean for different people. Mediating factors which may influence this meaning are considered in an attempt to reach a fuller understanding of the implications of unemployment for the individual.

THE FUNCTIONS OF WORK

Work in modern society serves many functions in that it provides outcomes that have the potential to satisfy a number of personal needs.

Work is a source of income

The classical concept of economic man suggests that this is the only reason for work, that men and women are motivated solely to maximize their material well-being. If this were an adequate description of people's motivation to work then it would be reasonable to assume that a person would cease working once material needs were satisfied. Testing this hypothesis Morse and Weiss (1955) asked over 400 men 'If by some chance you inherited enough money to live comfortably without working, do you think that you would work anyway or not? Eighty per cent of the total population questioned, and over 90 per cent of all those between the ages of twenty-one and thirty-four, replied that they *would* continue working. Brown (1954) investigated what actually happened to those who were the recipients of large, unexpected sums of money. He considered three London factory workers who won sums of money on the football pools, which, suitably invested, would have provided sufficient income for them to live comfortably for the rest of their lives. In fact, after only a short period of leisure, they all returned to work, two of them to highly repetitive jobs and one to a job as a fitter. These findings point to the importance of other functions or outcomes of work.

Work is a form of activity

A number of researchers have pointed to the importance of work in fulfilling the need to be active. Neff (1968), for example, states that one of the chief reasons given for wanting to work by people who are vocationally disabled is that work will alleviate their chronic conditions of boredom and inactivity. Work roles require the expenditure of energy in the form of physical or mental activity. Vroom (1964) states that all general theories of behaviour postulate that dissatisfaction results from the expenditure of energy and notes that the principle of 'least effort' has received considerable support from research using animals. Many experiments have shown that if animals are given two or more paths to the same goal, each involving a different level of energy expenditure, they will learn to choose the path involving least effort. However, the complete opposite – that the expenditure of effort is basically satisfying – has been demonstrated by other experiments. It has been found, for example, that rats will run in an activity wheel for periods in proportion to the time they were restricted. Vroom comments:

'It is not easy to reconcile the idea that activity reduces some aversive state which is produced by inactivity with the notion that activity increases some aversive state which is reduced only by inactivity. Each of these assumptions directly controverts the other. Probably neither is a complete statement of the unlearned affective consequences of energy expenditure. Conceivably there is some optimal level of activity. Lower amounts are unpleasant and tend to result in an increase in activity level, and higher amounts, as in fatigue, are also unpleasant and tend to result in a decrease in activity level.' (Vroom 1964:34)

The men in the Morse and Weiss study gave a number of reasons for wanting to continue working which could be interpreted in terms of a need to be active. Thirty-two per cent indicated that work kept them occupied and interested, 10 per cent that work kept them healthy and was good for them, 4 per cent said that without work they would feel bored and 10 per cent that without work they would not know what to do with their time. They indicated that they could not be idle. It would appear, therefore, that people do prefer to be active and that work provides them with that opportunity.

Work structures time

It determines at what time people have to get out of bed, how long they will be away from home and how they will spend their time during the day. It also provides structure over longer periods. It differentiates weekends and holidays from working days and provides many with a timetable for progressing through a career. As mentioned elsewhere in this book many of the people we talked to found that loss of work was very disorienting because it undermined the way they structured their lives. Jahoda (1979) illustrates this by describing what happened in an Austrian village in the 1930s when a factory closed down. She found that unemployed men lost their sense of time. When asked at the end of a day what they had done during it, they seemed unable to describe their activities. 'Real' time only appeared to enter their descriptions at the biologically incisive points, getting up, eating, going to bed, but the rest was vague and nebulous. She found that activities such as fetching wood from the shed, which could not have consumed more than a few minutes, were recorded as if they had filled the whole morning. None the less, the women complained that their menfolk were unpunctual for meals.

In Chapter 7 we note that one of the ways that the search for work, even if unsuccessful in terms of securing another job, can help the unemployed, is that it provides them with something to do and provides them with the opportunity to begin structuring their own time and developing their own schedules.

Work is a source of creativity and mastery

Hendrick (1943) postulates a work principle which suggests that pleasure in work is a consequence of the gratification of the instinct to master, or alter, the environment. He suggests that work is primarily motivated by the need for efficient use of the muscular and intellectual tools, regardless of what secondary needs, self-preservation, aggressive or sexual, a work performance may also satisfy. He calls this thesis the work principle; the principle that primary pleasure is sought by efficient use of the central nervous system for the performance of well-integrated ego functions which enable the individual to control or alter his or her environment.

Neff (1968) suggests that some people try to satisfy, through work, the need to be creative. In this context there can be more than one form of 'creativity'. At one level creativity may be synonymous with novelty; the rearrangement of traditional components into a new or unique pattern. He notes that creativity generally strikes us as a form of human activity that is quite idiosyncratic, expressive of the unique qualities of a particular person. At another level, however, creativity might be defined as the creation of an additional unit of something which is quite familiar. Neff argues, for example, that the typical industrial worker can be engaged in creative activity, and it is only when the process of automation proceeds so far that his connection with production becomes entirely attenuated that this opportunity is lost.

Creative activity stimulates people and provides for them the opportunity of feeling that they have achieved something. Work, therefore, can be meaningful because it is an area which enables the individual to create or explore something new or to master some part of the environment.

Work provides an opportunity for social interaction

Herzberg *et al.* (1957) reviewing fifteen studies which involved over 28,000 workers, found that the most frequently mentioned source of satisfaction was the 'social aspect of the job'. In the Morse and Weiss study 31 per cent of the respondents who said they would continue working indicated that if they did not work they would miss the people they knew at or through work. People need to feel they have a place in their group and that they have at least some affectionate relationships with others. The gregarious nature of man and the tendency to find social relationships satisfying has long been recognized. Work, especially in urban communities, can be an important source of social contacts and, as noted in Chapter 8, people bereft of work in such communities often experience a feeling of social isolation.

Work is a source of identity

The erosion of many traditional marks of identity emphasizes the importance of work and occupation as a source of identity. In small rural communities people have roots. They are known and identified as members of this or that family, as people who have special attitudes, interests, and skills, as people who spend their time in particular ways and mix with a certain set of friends. They are also known in terms of what they do, have done, and have not done. They are known for what they are. However, as communities grow and become more complex this full and intimate sense of identity tends to be lost. Each individual may relate with a variety of other people during each day. A large proportion of these relationships may only be brief encounters which do not offer either party the opportunity of gathering the data they would require in order to really get to know the other. Consequently relationships tend to assume a more ephemeral character and the job a person does tends to assume a greater significance in identifying the kind of person he or she is. The doctor is identified as a doctor by her friends, golf partners, and others and not only by her patients. To know that a person is a doctor enables others to make a wide range of assumptions as to the kind of person she is, her educational background, income, life-style, etc.

A person's occupation has become an important indicator of

status. Not only does it influence the status that is attributed to
the worker, it may also influence the status that is attributed to
the worker's family. In many households the father is the only
worker in paid employment outside the home. He is, therefore,
the link between two social systems, the home and work. Dyer
(1956) found that among blue-collar families, there was a high
correlation between the feelings of the father about his work and
the feelings his family had about his work. This was indicative of
communication and consensus within the family about the
father's job. The family was a major reference group for the
father. Consequently, dissatisfaction on the part of the family had
a significant influence on the father's attitudes and activities on
the job. Dyer also found that in their relationships outside the
family, all family members were aware of the relative status of the
father's occupation. Where this was low there was a general
dissatisfaction and a desire for the father to have a job with higher
prestige.

Unemployment undermines the individual's status and dam-
ages self-esteem when a person becomes dependent upon others,
or the State for support. Following Argyris' (1957) thesis that the
normal developmental pattern for the individual is one of growth
from total dependence towards independence, it is understand-
able that enforced dependence is not welcomed by the typical
mature person in contemporary society. This dependence often
produces feelings that they have failed and that they are disgraced
in the eyes of their family and others.

Finally, work gives to a person a sense of purpose

Whatever his or her occupation the worker feels needed. A
person's contribution to producing goods or providing services
forges a link between the individual and the society of which he
or she is a part. Work roles are not the only roles which offer the
individual the opportunity of being useful and contributing to
the community but, without doubt, for the majority they are the
most central roles and consequently people deprived of the
opportunity to work often feel useless and report that they lack a
sense of purpose.

THE INDIVIDUAL'S AFFECTIVE RESPONSE TO WORK

While work can serve many functions each individual may experience work differently. It can have different meanings for different people. Some will find that it provides them with precisely the identity, income, opportunity to associate with others, sense of purpose, and so forth which they desire. Others may feel that their job offers them little over and above an inadequate source of income. The 'meaning' of work is the affective response, or the feelings attributed to work as opposed to the 'functions' that work can serve for the individual.

Morse and Weiss suggest that the meaning of work for the individual is affected by the general type of work performed and by the kind of person he or she is. They suggest that for many people in middle-class occupations, working represents something interesting to do, having a chance to accomplish things and the opportunity to engage in a purposeful activity, whereas those in working-class occupations may view working as virtually synonymous with activity, the alternative to which is to lie around being bored and restless. In terms of job content they suggest that professional, managerial, and sales jobs concern symbols and meanings. Furthermore, the middle-class job imposes a responsibility for an outcome, for successful sales, successful operation of departments, or successful handling of legal cases. For a person in a middle-class occupation life without working would be less purposeful, stimulating, and challenging. They go on to suggest that the content of working-class jobs, on the other hand, concerns activity. Working-class occupations emphasize work with tools, operation of machines, lifting and carrying, and the individual is probably oriented to the effort rather than the end. Therefore, life without working becomes life without anything to do. Differences in the meaning attributed to work in various occupations may not only reflect job content but also the kind of person attracted into these occupations. They suggest that to some extent, at least, there may be selection into occupations so that the person going into a middle-class job has a different social background from one going into a working-class job. One might also argue that they have or develop a different self-concept in which work assumes a special place.

It is possible that, as Morse and Weiss suggest, both the nature of the job and the nature of the job holders operate together to produce a similarity of orientation towards the place of work in life among people in the same general type of job. Work may be more of an end in itself for some people and more of a means to an end for others.

Orzack (1959) found evidence to support this view. He studied a group of nurses and compared his findings with Dubin (1956), who studied a group of industrial workers. Particularly significant were his findings about work as a central life interest. Work was valued more as a near 'total way of life' by the professional workers than by the industrial workers. Nearly 80 per cent of all nurses felt about work in this way, whereas only just less than 25 per cent of industrial workers thought work was their central life interest.

Morse and Weiss asked those who had indicated that they would continue working even if they did not need the money whether they would continue to do the same kind of work. More than 60 per cent of the people in middle-class occupations said they would continue in their present jobs whereas only 34 per cent of those in working-class occupations replied in this way. While still wanting to work they indicated a preference for a different kind of job. In other words their attachment to working was stronger than their attachment to the job.

The status a person acquires from working is partly attributable to his or her particular job and partly attributable to the fact that he or she holds a job. Bakke (1940) has shown that those who work receive more respect than those who do not and Neff (1968) has observed that the professional who deals with the problems of the handicapped is frequently impressed by the high evaluation placed on work by those who are prevented from performing it.

Work may have different meanings for different people, but as well as these different meanings it also has an important and shared meaning for most people in society. Being a member of the work force, enjoying the status of worker, leads to considerable positive re-inforcement and satisfaction irrespective of the nature of the job or the immediate satisfactions that can be derived from the actual performance of the job. The protestant work ethic is still with us but in disguised form. It has been secularized. Work is no longer a religious duty leading to fulfilment in the here and now. The ideology that work is a central part of life is reinforced for young people through their early socialization. The home, the school, and the media encourage them to get on, to work hard, and to seek a career. Later in life the person without work is seen, and quickly learns to see himself or herself, as a second-class citizen with little status in society and with few opportunities to find fulfilment.

As mentioned in Chapter 1, 'employment' signifies more than a work activity. It is a social relationship. This needs to be borne in mind when considering measures designed to ameliorate the effects of loss of employment presented in Chapters 8 and 9. For example, some work creation schemes may provide substitute work activity but may fail to be perceived in terms of a purposeful relationship and therefore may be regarded as an imperfect substitute for loss of employment.

ATTITUDES TOWARD LOSS OF WORK

Attitudes towards loss of work can vary. Some people may have a positive attitude towards redundancy because they see it in terms of gain, as a means of closing the gap between their ideal world and the world as it is. Others may see it in terms of widening the gap. They may see problems rather than opportunities and therefore be disposed to view the transition negatively, in terms of loss. Kelly (1980) has developed this simple gain-loss model into a more sophisticated gain-loss-attachment-detachment (GLAD) model by adding a cognitive, attachment-detachment, dimension to the traditional affective gain-loss model. He suggests that where a person anticipates that he or she will receive more of existing outputs or some completely new outputs (pay, status, leisure time, etc.) as a result of the transition, it can be described in terms of a process of attachment. On the other hand where the person anticipates that he or she will receive less of some existing outputs the transition can be described as a process of detachment. By integrating this attachment-detachment perspective with the more traditional gain-loss model Kelly produces a theoretical framework which presents four different orientations to transition:

(1) *Attachment gain*, where the individual perceives the transition as closing the gap between his or her ideal world and the world as it is. The transition is seen as resulting in the receipt of more of some existing outputs that are desired and/or receiving some completely new output that is also desired.
(2) *Detachment gain*, where again the individual perceives the

transition as closing the gap between his or her ideal world and the world as it is. In this case the transition is seen as resulting in the receipt of less of some output that is not desired.

(3) *Attachment loss*, where the individual perceives the transition as widening the gap between his or her ideal world and the world as it is. Here the transition is seen as resulting in the receipt of more of some existing outputs that are not desired and/or some new outputs that are also not desired.

(4) *Detachment loss*, where the individual perceives the transition as widening the gap between his or her ideal world and the world as it is. In this case the transition is seen as resulting in the receipt of less of some output that is desired.

Kelly used this model to examine attitudes towards loss of work through retirement of 223 managers aged between forty and sixty-four who worked for an international manufacturing company in England. He found that the transfer from work to retirement was seen largely in terms of attachment and gain, although some did see it as involving both attachment and detachment and both gain and loss. However, only 6 per cent had a totally detachment orientation and only 10 per cent saw it in terms of an overall loss. The frequency with which different outcomes were mentioned by managers and the affective responses associated with them are shown in *Table 4(1)*.

These responses show that retirement is a very personal experience. Two people can view the same outcome very differently. For example 18 per cent of the managers stated that retirement would mean less routine; 12 per cent saw this in favourable terms (detachment-gain) whereas 6 per cent saw it unfavourably in terms of loss of an ordered and disciplined life (detachment-loss).

When examining *Table 4(1)* it is important to bear in mind that those statements reflect responses to anticipated and not actual loss of work. Some of the people interviewed were twenty years away from retirement. Also the anticipated loss of work investigated by Kelly was retirement rather than redundancy. Retirement may be a more acceptable transition than redundancy because it normally occurs at the end of a working life when the individual moves from one socially acceptable status to another. The worker who is made redundant on the other hand moves from the status of worker to the less acceptable status of un-

Table 4(1)　*Perceptions of retiring: a summary*

	attachment	%	detachment	%
F **A** **V** **O** **U** **R** **A** **B** **L** **E**	increased leisure time	86	less pressure/frustration associated with work	26
	increased time with wife and family	44	less routine	12
	adopting a new life-style	28	less responsibility	4
	new work opportunities	23	less travel	3
	increased opportunities to satisfy own needs	21	less social relationships	1
	extending existing and developing new relations	16		
	increased opportunity to move house	10		
	increased relaxation	9		
	new financial situation	7		
	increased awareness of ageing	5		
	increased time	5		
U **N** **F** **A** **V** **O** **U** **R** **A** **B** **L** **E**	adopting a new life-style	24	less income	43
	increased financial problems	22	less social relations	34
	increased awareness of age	13	less mental stimulation	21
	increased time	5	less status	8
	increased time with wife and family	4	less routine	6
	car purchase problems	3	less fitness and health	5
	increased pressure to move house	3	less responsibility	4
	increased leisure time	1	less travel	4
	new work opportunities	1	loss of company car	4
			less pressure associated with work	2

Note: This table summarizes the relative frequencies of statements made by the 223 managers.

employed worker. Indeed an analysis of much of the literature on unemployment suggests that it is overwhelmingly seen in terms of both detachment- and attachment-loss and rarely in terms of gain.

An unemployed textile worker we interviewed in Bradford talked about his inability to get a job and described his loss of purpose. 'I never used to give it much thought before but I don't know where I am going any more or what's the point of life.'

An ex-steel worker interviewed in a recent radio programme talked about his need for something to do and occupy his time, 'What does one do with oneself? Well, I woke up, looked at the paper, looked at what's on TV, anything that can occupy my mind and then I wait to go to bed. Well, that is not what I recognize as life. It's terrible.' Another unemployed steelworker who had received more than £10,000 compensation when he had lost his job said, 'If I had my way they could have their £10,000 back and I would go back to my job because I think the job was worth it.'

Our interviews with unemployed men and women in the Leeds/Bradford area highlighted the feeling of deprivation associated with the loss of outcomes from work. In other words, they saw the transition largely in terms of detachment-loss. They missed the feeling of being one of the team, of having people outside the family and neighbourhood to talk to, the politics and the intrigue of the workplace, and the gossip about people and events. They also missed the need to make decisions and the feeling of having to meet targets or quotas. One man doing a fairly routine job talked about how he had structured his day by keeping track of how much he had earned.

The greatest source of attachment-loss was linked with the extra leisure time they had and the increased time available to be with their spouse and family. While these outcomes were largely seen in terms of attachment-gain in Kelly's study, we found the unemployed we interviewed did not share this view. We found also that negative attitudes towards being at home were shared by both men and women. The feeling of being 'trapped by four walls' appeared to be most keenly felt by a woman who had restarted her career after several years of being a happy and fulfilled mother and housewife. After establishing her children at school she had 'discovered a new world at work', and begun to think of herself as 'capable of doing things I had never considered'. These negative attitudes towards the free time connected with unemployment are echoed by Ginsberg et al. (Sofer 1970) when they observed that:

'What is a pleasure to the employed man – to be at home with his family – is a burden to the unemployed. With no job to report to, and no place in particular to go, the man who had previously been at home only evenings and weekends was now constantly underfoot.'

While the overall orientation towards unemployment, of most of the people we talked to, was one of attachment- and detachment-loss (and especially the latter), that is, they saw it in terms of losing outcomes they valued and acquiring outcomes they did not want, there were a few, but only a few, who voiced occasional detachment- and attachment-gain comments which indicated that they had either left things behind that they were glad to get away from, for example, a particular supervisor, or that they had acquired new outcomes that they valued. One man told us about how he had always wanted to work for himself but had never dared take the risk. Redundancy had lifted the burden of making the disturbing decision of whether or not to give up his job and pension. Fineman (1979) also found that unemployment was seen as a detachment-gain by some people and reports that some of his subjects saw redundancy as a release from a difficult or stressful job.

Usually, people who hold positive attitudes towards unemployment are in a small minority. However, Little (1976) reports some surprising findings that are worthy of mention. He interviewed 100 unemployed male technical-professionals during the aerospace defence electronics recession in early 1972 and found that for many, unemployment was less stressful than expected. An unusually high proportion of his sample (48 per cent), expressed a positive attitude towards job loss. Only a minority of this group, 13 per cent, described their reason for having a positive attitude to unemployment in terms of detachment-gain, as a welcome relief from the stressful demands of work. The rest described their reasons in terms of attachment-gain. In spite of being made redundant, 24 per cent expressed a feeling of general optimism concerning their futures. They did not expect to remain out of work for long and referred to colleagues who had left the company and 'made out better financially and emotionally'. A further 13 per cent emphasized an expansion of their interests and an involvement in things, for example, politics, which they did not have time for before. A smaller group, 7 per cent, referred to the transition as providing a needed stimulus or challenge. 'It makes you think. It wakes you out of your lethargy.' The largest group, 34 per cent, described unemployment as representing an opportunity. 'I've been wanting to get out of it [electrical engineering] anyway. Now I've got time to find something I want to do.' 'I didn't like it at my last job. Maybe this is a chance to think about getting into a new career.' Little notes that, as in the example quoted above from our own interviews, many of his subjects had been having doubts about whether they were in the right field prior to being made redundant. While they desired a change they saw the risks as being too great and were glad when the lay-off made the decision to quit for them.

MEDIATING FACTORS

This large positive response to being laid-off deserves further examination. Little suggests that there were a number of factors which may have contributed to this response. One of the most important of these may have been that this group of technical professionals were able to view their employment as a career rather than as a job. Job loss could therefore be rationalized as a 'normal break' in their career. The cosmopolitan (Gouldner 1968) orientation of professionals to their careers is echoed by Perucci and Gerstl (1969) who note that the organizational attachment of the engineer does not involve a career-long affiliation to one firm. Rather, there is considerable mobility between organizations. This attempt to sustain their self-image by regarding unemployment as a career 'break' may have been aided by the high probability of obtaining other work. Many sectors of the economy were still buoyant, and those who were laid-off had a general professional training which gave them the option of either seeking similar work to that which they had lost or looking downwards in the occupational structure for temporary work or even an entrée to a new career. An analysis of Little's data shows that it was those in the middle, as opposed to the beginning or end of their careers, who showed the greatest tendency to view job loss positively. One might expect that these would be the people who might, for professional-career reasons, such as widening their experience or seeking promotion, be most inclined to change jobs anyway.

Another mediating factor was the extensive publicity, at the time of the lay-offs, that the media gave to the professional unemployment crisis. This may have helped sustain the individual's self-image, because it deflected the blame for unemployment away from the individual. Furthermore, many of their colleagues, who comprised an important reference group, were faced with the same predicament.

Three other factors were mentioned by Little. The first of these was that among this group idleness did not appear to be the widespread and serious problem that other studies seemed to predict. Many of Little's subjects reported that they enjoyed having more time to read and indulge in other hobbies and he found that those who experienced greatest difficulty with idleness were the ones who tended to be less likely to have a positive attitude towards job loss. The second of these factors was that those who were in the strongest financial position were also inclined to view job loss positively, and finally those who evidenced low satisfaction with their previous job were most likely to have a positive attitude to job loss.

When unemployment challenges the assumptions the individual makes about his or her identity as a person, threatens the continued availability of the many outcomes desired from work, and confronts the individual with new outcomes he or she may not desire, then attitudes towards loss of work are likely to be negative and the process of adjustment to the transition from work to unemployment is likely to reflect the process discussed in Chapters 2 and 3. However, where unemployment does not represent such a challenge or threat and when many of the new outcomes are desired and seen as a gain, then the individual's attitude towards unemployment is likely to be more positive and his or her reaction to the change in circumstances may deviate from the normal pattern discussed above.

It is possible to identify groups of people who might exhibit atypical responses to loss of work. They might include, for example, some school leavers, the financially well off, those who see themselves as 'legitimately' unemployed, and others.

School leavers

Most school leavers have not experienced work in an occupational sense, but they will have formed expectations about work and working. There will be those whose background and early socialization have encouraged the development of a public persona in which the occupational self-concept forms an important part. There will be others who have experienced very little anticipatory occupational socialization. The former group will be those whose life plans and self-images embrace work as a central theme whereas the latter group will include those who, while aspiring to get some sort of work, are likely to have less well clearly defined career aspirations and are more likely to 'see what's around' when they leave school. The experience of unemployment for this group is likely to require few changes in the assumptions they make about how to relate to the world around them. The former group, on the other hand, may well have to cope with the loss of something they have never had but which they assumed they would have. Their assumptive world embraces the concept of themselves as worker. If they are not to realize this anticipated goal they will have to make some fundamental changes in the assumptions they make about how they will relate to their future life space.

Relevant to both groups will be their recent experience of extended leisure time. This experience might influence their ability to cope with the problems associated with the free time that accompanies unemployment. For both these reasons, therefore, the psychological effects of unemployment may be less powerful for some school leavers than for those who were previously employed on a full-time basis. Furthermore, the financial effects of unemployment are likely to be less traumatic. While compared with those in work the school leaver may be 'badly off', and would naturally like more money than he or she gets through social security payments in order to buy the luxuries of youth, the actual change in financial circumstances following unemployment will be much less than for someone who has been working, and will be ameliorated by the limited extent to which he or she has to contribute to the family budget. In the sense that the school leaver is not *the* 'breadwinner' for the family and has less financial responsibility for others he or she will be under less psycho-economic pressure. One mother of an unemployed school leaver told us that they didn't take anything for his upkeep, 'We've kept him for sixteen years and we'll manage till he gets a job of his own. He needs his "social" for his clothes and motor bike.'

Finally, the extent to which the views of others will affect the unemployed school leaver's self-image will be a function of the individual's reference group and the attitudes of significant others. This could depend on the general level of youth unemployment in the area. In an area of high youth unemployment the large numbers of similarly unemployed young people may help to lessen the individual stigma attached to unemployment and will perhaps enable the individual to sustain an assumptive world commensurate with his or her self image. This is implicitly expressed in a report by Nally:

> 'Outside a nearby pub there was a constantly changing gaggle of young West Indians with nothing to do but while away the hours chatting up each other and trying to cadge cigarettes. A girl said, "Who wants me? You tell me and I'll run after them. It's not that easy, see. You work round here you're an exception."'
>
> (Nally 1979)

Nally's case material supports the view that school leavers may follow an atypical cycle of adjustment moving much more quickly than most unemployed people to a fatalistic acceptance of the status quo. Thus a youth said, 'I'd not expected much when I left last year, but I felt by the end of the year that there must be something for me. I'm knackered with hearing them say there's nothing. So I don't expect any more' (Nally 1974).

The fear of this acceptance is expressed by a father of an unemployed youth when he said:

> 'It's getting far enough. I'd like to see him getting a job now. I'm frightened of him getting used to it, that's what I'm frightened of, that's the danger, because I've witnessed it myself. He's been finished a year this week.'
>
> (Marsden 1975:204)

Financially well off

When people lose their job they also lose their means of earning a living. While the initial period of unemployment is, at the time of writing, cushioned in the UK by the availability of an earnings related supplement which is added to unemployment benefit, there is evidence that many of the unemployed feel that somehow these benefits are not quite 'legitimate'. As one person we spoke to said, 'The money's not too bad at the moment, I'm still on earnings related, but I just don't feel I've earned it,' and another who had been unemployed for two months, and whom we knew quite well, simply kept putting off claiming free school meals for

his children. He was prepared to get into debt with the electricity
board to the extent of having his supply disconnected, but still
felt that in some way it was not 'right' to accept free school meals
for his children. After a while, however, the cushioning effect of
earnings related supplement (available for only six months),
savings, severance pay, etc., begin to dwindle and the financial
pressures increase. These pressures intensify during the intermediate phase of the adjustment cycle and contribute to the
depression and anxiety typically experienced by the unemployed.

Increased financial pressures make it difficult to sustain the old
life-style and associated images of self. 'Substitute' work also has
to be abandoned. One man told us, 'I'll have to sell the car. You
know, that'll be a great loss as I used to spend hours *working* on
that machine,' and Gould reports a comment almost identical to
one made to us by one of our interviewees:

> 'You have to do the garden, decorating even when you can't
> afford to decorate. I've stripped the landing, but we don't know
> how we're going to pay for it. It didn't really want stripping,
> but it's just something to do. You have to keep your mind
> occupied.'   (Gould and Kenyon 1972:40)

However, those who have some form of financial security
which they can regard as 'legitimate' may be able to maintain
their old life-style and hold on to many of the assumptions they
make about how they relate to the world around them. This is
illustrated by a fifty-three-year-old unemployed medical representative whom we interviewed and who had been made redundant
six months previously. He had been well paid and had managed
to save a considerable proportion of his earnings. He had also
received generous severance pay because he had worked in the
same firm for twenty-seven years. Furthermore, his wife worked,
which meant that there was another source of income for the
family. This person, unlike many others who had been unemployed for six months, was still optimistic. He still had his
car, had plenty of hobbies, 'I could retire tomorrow in terms of
hobbies,' and still paid for his son to go to a private school. Thus
the lack of financial pressure seemed to have had an ameliorating
effect on the psychological consequences of unemployment. His
self-esteem was still high and he was optimistic and involved
with life. It was the financially well off in Little's study who
tended to see loss of work in more positive terms but, as Morse

and Weiss confirmed, work is not only a source of income. Financial security may cushion the effects of unemployment but the underlying problem may remain. Our medical representative recognized this, 'What I'll think in six months' time when the money's gone down a bit and I still haven't got a job – well, who knows?'

Legitimate unemployment

The 'legitimately unemployed' are those who feel that, whilst their role and circumstances have changed, their self-esteem is not unduly threatened. They feel this way because they perceive, and they believe that others also perceive, that their transition from work to unemployment was legitimate. They were not to blame. Their predicament is a product of circumstances beyond their control. Either these circumstances left them with no choice or pointed to unemployment as the only real option. Consequently the element of humiliation often associated with loss of work is minimized. The individual can maintain his or her self-respect and can expect to receive the respect of others.

The sort of cases which would be included in this category are the disabled, parents of one-parent families, those made redundant near to retiring age, those who have to look after disabled or sick relatives, and even those, as in Little's study, who are able to explain to themselves and others their unemployed status as a natural career break that would have been sought in the near future even if it had not been imposed.

Legitimization of their unemployment does not mean that they do not experience the loss of outputs associated with work, but rather that the situation may allow them to maintain their self-respect. One single-parent father whose wife had died and who was caring for his eight children said, 'I'd rather be working. What kind of a life is this for a man, looking after the kids . . .? But I've got to do it. There's nobody else. It's the best way for the family' (Marsden 1975 : 175). A man we interviewed in a pub, who had been made redundant at sixty-three and who felt he had no chance of getting another job said, 'Well, it'll only be another year and a half and I'll be retired.' What was significant about this interview was the attitude of the regulars in the pub, who had been and still remained his main reference group outside work. Their attitude to his redundancy, which was expressed in front of the man, was that 'The bastards could have kept him on for another year,' and a former workmate, still employed by the firm said, 'He was a good worker, the bloke who's doing his job now is bloody rubbish.' About his new status as unemployed they commented, 'I mean it's just like he's retired. A lot of people retire before they are sixty-three, don't they?' In essence this 'cooling out' (Goffman 1952) was a factor which enabled the man to commence the process of re-evaluating his position in terms of an individually and socially legitimated framework.

Other mediating factors

In examining these groups who appear to deviate in a number of ways from the transitional cycle discussed earlier we have been trying to identify those factors which may account for these deviations. Thus for school leavers it was their lack of experience of having a life-style which wages permit, the existence of reference groups of similarly situated people, the availability of financial and psychological support from the family and so forth. For the financially well off it was the absence of financial pressures and the continuation of a life-style commensurate with an employed existence, and for the legitimately unemployed it was the publically and self-perceived legitimacy of their position which mitigated against the possible self and publically defined stigmatization.

A range of other mediating factors can be identified. The first of these is social support. Those who are able to retain membership of their pre-redundancy work groups, as for example when the whole group has been unemployed and where they still have the opportunity to associate together, may find that these groups provide both social support and companionship. Furthermore, as will be discussed in Chapter 9, family and social support, even when this is not linked with the companionship of people similarly displaced, can be an important mediating factor in its own right.

The availability and propensity to engage in alternative types of 'work' whilst unemployed may also produce a different reaction in individuals. Thus, using the time one is unemployed to gain additional training or education may lessen the effects of unemployment, as might the taking of unpaid work with some voluntary organization. Such activities may serve to reduce boredom, and, in terms of self- and public perception, symbolize a willingness to work and thus reduce the stigmatization associated with unemployment. One person we interviewed had recently been accepted for a TOPS course starting in three months time, and he told us that he had immediately made this clear to the lady behind the counter when he went to collect his unemployment benefit. 'She now knows that I'm not really unemployed, but just waiting until the course starts.'

Another factor which may affect at least the initial reaction to unemployment, is the manner in which the person came to be unemployed. It could be that there is a difference in the psychological reaction to unemployment depending on whether the person was asked to retire early, made redundant, left voluntarily, or given the sack. Whilst all four deprive the individual of the means of maintaining a particular self-image, actually getting the sack, one might predict, would be a greater threat to self-image than early retirement, redundancy or voluntary leaving. Of the people we interviewed, the two who had been sacked had established reasons for the sackings, which seemed to represent an attempt to show that their dismissals were not a reflection on themselves. 'The foreman was puddled. I'd never dug a ditch with a JCB before, he shouldn't have set me on that job' (he had been sacked for poor work), and, 'The boss was pissed and he was in a temper. He was looking for someone to have a go at. People like that shouldn't be in charge of people' (he didn't actually explain why he had been sacked).

Job satisfaction and the meaning of work for the individual may also be a mediating factor. Saleh and Otis (1963) found that workers who expressed intrinsic satisfaction with work looked at retirement less favourably than context-oriented workers. Little's study found that the level of job satisfaction was related to attitudes towards loss of work, and an interesting paper by Maclean (1977) discusses chronic welfare dependency from the perspective of the satisfactions associated with the relative outcomes of working and not working. Maclean argues that there are people for whom work induces feelings of anxiety and helplessness and provides few, if any, satisfactions. He observes that for some people menial employment demands long hours, hard work and results in little advancement, recognition or financial reward. At the same time such people may be faced with inflation, a growing family, and increased indebtedness which makes their earning power even more inadequate. These conditions create stress and tension in the home and further decrease satisfaction with life in general. For such people unemployment and the welfare payments that go along with this status may represent a welcome relief, reduce their anxiety and increase their feeling of predictability and control. In other words, unemployment may be perceived almost totally in terms of detachment and attachment gain. Rehabilitation may not hold much value for them because any attempt to re-establish them in employment may threaten their new-found sense of stability.

In many cases these mediating factors may combine and operate together in order to influence attitudes towards work and employment. Thus, in the previous example, several variables might have been important. Low job satisfaction, a better financial status associated with unemployment, and social support from a reference group which does not value work highly may combine to produce a more positive attitude to unemployment. More research, adopting a multivariate approach, would greatly improve our understanding of this area.

The ambitious

In examining the cases of various groups and individuals who appear to deviate in some way from the transitional cycle discussed earlier we have tended to focus on mediating factors which damp down some of the negative effects of unemployment. There are, however, cases where the transitional cycle may occur more quickly and with an increased intensity in the amplitude of the phases. One example concerns people who are high achievers and who have had an extended period of success in fulfilling their ambitions through work. The case of the rising executive given by Seligman (1975) and quoted in Chapter 3, is of this type, and while the explanation for the move to depression is given in terms of Seligman's theory of helplessness, the intensity of the depression and the speed of the move to the depression may be more explicable in terms of the meaning of work for the individual and the centrality of work to the self-concept.

It is possible that for those individuals who invest unusually large parts of their time and energy in work, the experiences that such efforts produce will be important in terms of maintaining their self-image. Through successful occupational achievement this self-image is reinforced and becomes a central and essential part of the self. For such people the loss of the means of sustaining this central and significant view of themselves may be traumatic. In the same way that the extent of grief or reaction to bereavement can be a function of the emotional importance of the lost person to the bereaved, so with unemployment, the extent of the reaction to loss of work may be a function of the importance of work to the individual. Work assumes a central role in the assumptive worlds of the ambitious and successful and probably provides the major experiences through which their self-image is maintained. Consequently, the loss of this role requires an essential and fundamental change in both their assumptive worlds and in their self-image. Bakke illustrates this well when commenting on the reactions to unemployment in Greenwich of the most ambitious men:

> 'Robbed of a job, the difference in ability as between in-
> dividuals, has only one chance of expression – more or less
> initiative in finding work. Until work is found, the greater
> efficiency, the better attitudes to work – these are of no value.
> The job is the medium in which these qualities acquire sig-
> nificance. Without this job they are useless. . . . But this added
> aggressiveness in looking for work is just the factor which
> throws a man, if unsuccessful, against rebuff after rebuff, and
> the sensitiveness to the importance of his place as a worker will
> cause him to get disheartened more quickly than the man who
> has less sensitiveness on this point.
>
> I was not surprised, therefore, to find amongst the men with
> whom I associated for several months that the most ambitious
> lost heart more quickly. The quality that on the job leads to
> rapid achievement of greater satisfaction, off the job, leads to
> rapid retreat into hopelessness and discontent, despair and
> even sullenness. The incentive to work hard, the desire to
> push ahead, the ambition to perfect one's technique, these are
> basic qualities for satisfaction at work. They are just the
> qualities that make it hardest for a man to be out of work.'
>
> (Bakke 1933:71)

CHANGES IN ATTITUDE

Attitudes towards work and unemployment are not static. They change over time. If the individual is to adjust to the prospect of being unemployed indefinitely, or come to terms with the idea that he or she may never work again, the individual has to let go of the image of him- or herself as a worker and has to develop purposes and objectives in non-work terms. As mentioned in Chapter 3, one way of analysing this process of adjustment is in terms of cognitive dissonance. Little suggests that cognitive dissonance probably accounts for a certain amount of the positive attitude toward job loss which he found in his study of the technical professional. Most of the men he interviewed gave an impression that they regarded themselves as competent and valuable people in the field. Being unemployed was clearly inconsistent with this self-image, therefore, he suggests, to resolve this inconsistency they might have been inclined to emphasize the positive aspects of unemployment in an attempt to convince others and themselves that losing their jobs was in line with what they really wanted. The greater the duration of unemployment the greater may be the pressure to seek consistency by changing attitudes towards work and unemployment.

Alfano (1973) constructed a scale to measure the individual's attitude toward work and found, using a cross-sectional research design, that there was a clear relationship between length of unemployment and attitudes towards work. He reported that attitudes towards employment did not change in the first six months of unemployment and that the mean scores of those currently employed and those unemployed for between one and six months were essentially the same. However, the mean attitude score for those unemployed more than six months but less than eighteen months was substantially lower than the score for those currently employed and those unemployed for more than eighteen months showed a further substantial drop.

MEDIATING FACTORS AND THE MEANING OF WORK AND UNEMPLOYMENT

This chapter has looked at the functions of work and the special meaning that work may have for different people. It has also examined how people anticipate and experience the transition in cognitive and affective terms, and, in addition, it has been noted that these reactions may change, especially as the duration of unemployment increases. Attention has been paid to mediating factors which can operate to influence the way in which the individual regards work and unemployment. The main point of examining these 'mediating influences' has been to show that while it is possible to describe a transitional cycle and give some psychological explanations of why most people will tend to follow such a cycle, when we are looking at individual cases there are a great many factors which may need to be taken into account in order to understand and explain a particular individual's reaction.

The following case illustrates this point in a particularly bizarre fashion, and also illustrates the cognitive, and emotional complexity, which makes prediction so much more difficult. The interviewee, a fifty-year-old former bricklayer, had been unemployed for a year. He started the interview by telling us that he was different from other people who were unemployed. 'I'm optimistic about the future.' He'd been sacked from his last job, but now couldn't get another job as he had to look after his mother who was dying. Also it had been discovered that he had a compound fracture in his foot, and that one leg was shorter than the other. Consequently he was now registered as disabled. The incident that had caused the disablement had occurred some time ago, but it was only after he had become unemployed that the fracture had been discovered, and that 'I shouldn't have been doing the job in the first place.' 'You see I can't do anything until my mother dies. I'd rather be behind a shop counter than at home, it's not in my nature.' (Repeated three times in thirty minutes.) The reason he said he was different from 'the others' was, 'I've got information.' When asked if he could tell us about this he said, 'There's going to be a major change in the world soon. I've known about this since 1961, but God had to wait for silicon chips. You see that's why I'm optimistic about the future.' When discussing his daily activity he said with venom that, 'I'm never bored, I do the gardening and all the housework for my mother', and later he said that, 'I live from day to day, I take it a day at a time.' Of particular note was the way he left the room after the interview. Whereas he had walked in, he limped out!

One way of looking at, and attempting to explain what had taken place in this interview was in terms of an individual seeking to maintain 'face' (Goffman 1955) in the light of what he might well have perceived as a threat to his present position and self-image. Whatever the explanation, an important factor that the interview brought home to us was that there is an enormous diversity of constructs that individuals can bring to bear in order to explain, understand, and cope with their unemployed predicament.

5 The health consequences of unemployment

'There is not enough research in the work setting to prove a cause and effect relationship between job stress and bad health. But practitioners dealing with health problems on a day to day basis generally feel that the correlational, case history, and anecdotal evidence is convincing.'

MARGOLIS AND KROES 1974:142

In attempting to arrive at some understanding of the consequences of job loss in terms of both physical and mental health we concur with the ideas expressed in the Margolis and Kroes quotation above. Whilst they were concerned to review the relationship between work and health, our view is that similar conclusions apply to the relationship between unemployment and health. Our aim, therefore, in this chapter is not to present certainties and proven cause-and-effect relationships, of which there are few. Rather, in the process of presenting some of the work that has been done in this area, it is to suggest possibilities, highlight probabilities, and in general to offer signposts towards ways of understanding the various consequences that unemployment might have for mental and physical well-being. Whilst research into the health consequences of unemployment is, at the present time, meagre, we feel that what evidence there is, is sufficient to support the proposition that some deterioration in health is a probable consequence of involuntary job loss. Before proceeding we shall put forward a model to provide a framework against which the findings from the research may be viewed. This model, proposed by French and Khan (1962), is used as the framework for research into the effects of the work role on physical and mental health and we feel it will serve the same purpose in examining the effects of unemployment on physical and mental health.

THE ISR MODEL

The ISR model (see *Figure 5(1)*) is used as a framework for research carried out under the auspices of the Institute for Social Research at the University of Michigan, and represents more a series of categories through which to examine the relevant factors which give rise to health conditions rather than a theory of the relationship between various factors and health conditions. As we start to fill in the categories with various sub-categories relevant to unemployment we will see how useful the model is in providing a framework within which to view the diverse case studies and research findings.

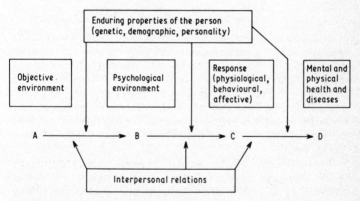

Figure 5(1) ISR model: the social environment and mental health

Source: Katz and Kahn 1978 : 584 (reproduced with the permission of John Wiley & Sons, Inc.).

Basically the model can be seen as a series of steps or links in a chain from the subjective circumstances of the individual, in this case the objective environment of a person's unemployed existence, through to the physical and mental health characteristics. The first link in the chain is between the objective circumstances and how these are viewed by the individual. The second link is between these perceptions and cognitions of the environment and the variety of physiological, behavioural, and effective responses to these perceptions and cognitions. The third and final link is between those various responses and the individual's physical and mental health. Each link in the chain is mediated by and modified by both the nature of the individual in terms of his or her genetic, demographic, and personality characteristics and also by the extent and nature of their interpersonal relationships.

As we have seen in the preceding chapters there are a variety of differing responses to the objective circumstances which face people when unemployed. In order to clarify the model and bring out the nature and complexity of the links we describe two cases which typically represent the experiences of many of the people we interviewed.

CASE I: MARY

Mary is a forty-six-year-old widow with two children aged ten and fourteen. She has worked as a skilled machine operator since the death of her husband six years ago. Her company laid her off as a result of a rationalization programme which resulted in the transfer of her work to another of their sites. She had been unemployed for ten months, during which time she has applied for many varied jobs without success. She has used up much of her savings and has tended to lose touch with most of her former workmates.

After getting over the 'shock' of the redundancy Mary felt that she would soon find another job again, given her good work record and level of skills. She now felt pessimistic about the possibility of gaining future employment, but still checked in the papers and wrote off occasionally for interviews. She felt after several interviews that her age was against her, but recently this view had been challenged as she had heard that two of her former workmates of the same age had got jobs that she had applied for. Because of her reduced financial circumstances she had been unable to buy the children as many clothes as she had done previously and felt that particularly her fourteen-year-old daughter was becoming resentful of the change. Whereas in the initial stages of her unemployment she had put a lot of effort into cleaning the house and also into decorating, she had now given up, partly because she felt it did not really need doing and partly because she felt she could not afford it.

She noticed that recently she had started to find it difficult to sleep, and often when she did she would wake up and worry for a long time until she eventually went off to sleep again. After getting the children off to school she would go back to bed and sleep for much of the morning, partly because she hadn't slept well during the night and partly because she could see no point in getting up. She had lost weight over the past three months and complained of severe bouts of depression. At times like these, she felt that the children just left her to get on with it, rather than made attempts to help her. In the end Mary went to the doctor who prescribed tranquillisers. He also sent her for tests to the local hospital as he suspected that Mary might have an ulcer.

CASE 2: MICK

Mick is a thirty-two-year-old married man with two children aged five and three. His wife is a teacher. Mick had been the personnel manager of a medium-sized organization. He had worked there since leaving university, and had been made redundant when the firm closed down. He had been unemployed for three months during which time he had applied for a variety of jobs and had been accepted for three. He had refused these as he had decided to wait for a job with more prospects. Mick felt that he had been getting into a rut in his previous job and also that promotion was a question of 'dead men's shoes'. He had been surprised about the firm's closure but had not been unduly worried as he felt he would easily be able to get another job. He had declined the jobs he had been offered partly because the money was no better than his previous job and partly because the prospects of promotion seemed about the same. Essentially he did not want to end up in the same rut as before. Mick had found the three months out of work interesting and felt that it had given him time to think about what he really wanted to do. Also he had spent quite a lot of time playing golf. With the redundancy payments and his wife's salary they had been no worse off financially, though he realized that he would have to take a job soon. His wife agreed that he should take his time finding a job that he would like rather than take the first one that came along, and was also quite happy to find that many of the household chores had been done when she came home from work. Mick's health was good and whilst he was starting to get a bit bored at times he was still enjoying his break.

Whilst both of the above cases are hypothetical in the sense that they are not descriptions of actual cases, nevertheless, they are based on the findings of our own interviews and those case studies and information reported in the literature. We shall use these case studies to explain the nature of the ISR model and to examine its usefulness in describing the processes of change that the individual might go through when unemployed.

ANALYSIS OF MARY

The first link in the chain is between Mary's objective environment and her psychological environment, that is between the objective conditions of her unemployment (e.g. time out of work, number of jobs applied for, level of income, etc.), and how she perceives and views these conditions. This link is powerfully mediated by the variety of idiosyncratic factors such as the nature of the support she receives from significant people in her environment and also by the nature and complexity of her psychological make up. (That is, by the nature of the enduring properties of the person and by the extent and nature of her interpersonal relationships.)

On the basis of the case study we can say that Mary's psychological environment is such that she is uncertain about both herself and her place in the world. Her original beliefs about getting employment quickly had had to be modified, and in turn these new beliefs which included her age as a key inhibiting factor in her search for employment, had also been subject to modification. Consequently, she is unclear about her own abilities and how these relate to her employment prospects. Further, she is starting to question the ways in which her children view her in terms of a breadwinner who is not providing as much as before. In other words, major changes in her view of herself and of her social world are necessitated by changes in her objective environment. Mary's responses to the above perceptions of her objective environment (that is, the link between her psychological environment and her physiological, behavioural, and effective states), are described in the case study in terms of weight loss, sleeplessness, anxiety, and depression. The final link between such responses and the physical and mental health consequences are also described in the case study in terms of the need to control the anxiety and depression and in the possible dietary disorder.

It should be remembered that these final links in the chain are also mediated (in the same way as the other links), by the personality and interpersonal circumstances of the individual. Another individual who perceives the situation in precisely the same way may respond quite differently.

ANALYSIS OF MICK

Whilst it is possible to describe Mick's perception of the future as being uncertain, this uncertainty is of a different order to that which affected Mary. In the first place it is self-imposed by the rejection of three jobs, and secondly, it is an uncertainty as to whether things will get better. That is, whether he will be able to find a job which will offer him greater satisfaction or whether things will remain largely as they were. The base line, therefore, of Mick's uncertainty is accepting a job similar to the one previously held on the same salary. Mick's perception of his environment is positively oriented and, as can be gathered from the case study, his interpersonal relationships are supportive of such a view. It would seem from the case study that Mick's response to unemployment is in terms of an opportunity to engage in activities which he found pleasurable and in terms of an opportunity to evaluate his life and consider his future in a positive way. It would also seem that there was no negative relationship between these responses and his physical and mental health.

We hope to have shown from these admittedly superficial cases that the ISR model can be useful in laying down a framework within which to view changes and health consequences that unemployed people may face. What should be clear from the preceding chapters and is perhaps more easily emphasized in the ISR model, is that the relationship between unemployment and, in the case of this chapter, health, is of an extremely high order of complexity.

In looking at the first link in the model (A→B) (*Figure 5(1)*) we could list a vast range of variables which make up an individual's objective environment: the time employed, the time unemployed, the reason for the unemployment, the level and type of unemployment in the area, the skills and abilities of the person, the financial circumstances, the commitments in terms of mortgages, loans, etc., the person's responsibilities in terms of other people dependent upon them, and so on. We could then list the variety of individual differences: the person's age, their previous biographies, personalities, world views and how these relate to their abilities to cope with unemployment, how they perceive their circumstances, and also their familial and social relationships, all of which differentially affect the way in which individuals come to form views of themselves and the circumstances in which they exist.

The relationship, then, between an individual's objective environment and the psychological environment is clearly complex, and the problem is further compounded when we realize that there is a similar level of complexity in the relationship (B→C) between the psychological environment and the individual's responses in terms of the physiological, behavioural and affective states. Finally, the last link in the chain (C→D) that between an individual's responses and his or her physical and mental health, is also characterized by this level of complexity.

The reason for making explicit the complexity of the relationship between unemployment and health is to provide a backcloth against which the researches, which we shall describe in this chapter, may be viewed. The first point is that much of the work that has been undertaken in this area has not been directly concerned with the relationship between unemployment and health *per se*, but rather with associated relationships such as between unemployment and self-esteem (e.g. Strange 1978), and unemployment and welfare (e.g. Stone 1971). Secondly, work on mental health and unemployment has tended to be concerned with factors involving the rehabilitation of people with mental health problems back into employment, rather than the mental health consequences of unemployment. In other words, the majority of work is within a framework of people being unemployed because of mental health problems rather than unemployment itself being one of the causes of those mental health problems. Thirdly, work that has been specifically aimed at examining the relationship between unemployment and health tends to be wary of making any causal connection. Thus Kasl, Gore, and Cobb conclude one paper on the relationship between job loss and changes in health as follows:

'These findings have convinced us that studying intensively and longitudinally the effects of *one* stressful life event such as job loss, is an exceedingly complex business. Different outcome variables may show strikingly different patterns of change and all appear sensitive to the characteristics of the person and of the social situation. Moreover the findings in this report as well as earlier reports dealing with physiological variables, show that the period of anticipation of the event can be at least as stressful as the event itself. Consequently, dating the onset of particular life events for particular individuals may not be a simple matter.'   (Kasl, Gore, and Cobb 1975:121)

Though concurring with the view expressed in this quotation, we nevertheless feel that whilst no conclusive evidence is available to substantiate a direct causal relationship between unemployment and health, if the diverse findings that there are, are taken together, then we believe there is enough evidence to alert people to the possible health consequences of unemployment. It is to these findings that we now turn.

LIFE CHANGE AND ILLNESS SUSCEPTIBILITY

As we have shown in the preceding chapters, job loss can be seen as a psycho-social transition which necessitates the giving up of one particular life space and assumptive world and the acceptance of another. The effects of events which require this readjustment of an individual's life space and assumptive world on his or her health has been investigated by a variety of authors in recent years.

This work started with Adolf Meyer, who developed the idea of plotting his patients' 'life-charts' (the record of significant events in their biographies). He was able to show that his patients were more likely to become ill soon after a cluster of significant life changes than would be expected by chance. Developing these ideas Harold G. Wolff was able to put forward evidence that, '"stressful events" by evoking psycho-physiological reactions played an important causative role in the natural history of many diseases' (Holmes and Masuda 1973:162).

Following on from the work of Meyer and Wolff, Thomas H. Holmes and his colleagues developed the Social Readjustment Rating Scale (SRRS) (Holmes and Rahe 1967). This scale was made up of forty-three life events. On the basis of their clinical experience they believed that these events were indicative of or required a significant change in the life of the individual, and were thus associated with some form of adaptive or coping behaviour on the part of the individual experiencing the event. Through an extensive research procedure they were able to rank the various life events and establish the relative significance of the events for people (see *Table 5(1)*). A large number of research studies have been conducted using the SRRS (see Holmes and Masuda 1973) and, whilst there are variations in the findings, the main conclusions appear to be that the magnitude of the life change is significantly related to the seriousness of the illness. What then is the relevance of these findings for job loss?

Table 5(1) *Selected life events from the Social Readjustment Rating Scale*

rank	life event	mean value
1	death of spouse	100
2	divorce	73
3	marital separation	65
6	personal injury or illness	53
8	fired at work	47
10	retirement	45
15	business readjustment	39
16	change in financial state	38
18	change to different line of work	36
19	change in number of arguments with spouse	35
21	foreclosure of mortgage or loan	30
22	change in responsibilities at work	29
28	change in living conditions	25
29	revision of personal habits	24
30	trouble with boss	23
31	change in work hours or conditions	20
34	change in recreation	19
38	change in sleeping habits	16

Source: Holmes and Rahe 1967:216.

Of those events included in the SRRS several could directly relate to or cluster around the condition of unemployment. In *Table 5(1)* we present a selection of the life events in the scale and include some of those we think significant for unemployment. The relevance of this line of work for the health consequences of job loss is based, firstly, on the fact that a considerable amount of research has shown that the onset of disease is related to the degree of life change an individual has to cope with, and secondly, that unemployment as we have shown in the

preceding chapters is a major life change for most people requir-
ing adaptive or coping behaviours in a whole range of areas in an
individual's life space. It would seem, therefore, that in considering the number of items on the SRRS which would relate to
unemployment, there would appear to be a reasonable indication
that life changes involved in unemployment could well be an
important factor in relation to the onset of illness in unemployed
people.

When it comes to examining the evidence for the relationship
between health and unemployment we find firstly, that little
research has been conducted in this area, and secondly, of the
research that has been done, it is often difficult to establish the
nature of the relationship. Thus Stone and Schlamp (1971), in
extensive research involving 1000 families, found that the 808
welfare cases as against the 392 non-welfare cases were more
likely to have medical problems, and also that, of the welfare
cases, those that had been on aid longest manifested the highest
percentage of illness. However, as Stone and Schlamp point out:

'Of the various handicaps that have been listed (social, economic, medical, and psychological), it is difficult to know how
many are present only as a result of the welfare dependency
experience itself.'

And:

'Whether viewed as organic or functional in character, illness
turns the individual back on himself and produces regressive
tendencies. Thus it might seem plausible that illness tends to
increase psychological dependency, on the other hand it is
equally plausible to suppose that a high degree of psychological
dependency may produce psychosomatic illness.'

(1971:236)

We might add that it is even more plausible that some form of
interdependent relationship exists between the psychological
and physiological states of the individual.

UNEMPLOYMENT AND HEALTH

Perhaps the most relevant research and the most detailed study of
the health consequences of unemployment is that carried out by
Stanislav Kasl and Sidney Cobb, aspects of which are reported in a

variety of papers (Kasl and Cobb 1970; 1971; Kasl, Cobb and Gore 1972; 1975; Cobb *et al.*, 1966; 1970). Basically, their study was a longitudinal investigation of the effects of job loss and the ensuing unemployment and/or job change experience on semi-skilled blue collar workers. These workers were thirty-five- to sixty-year-old married men, who had been made unemployed because of plant closure.

The study involved the collection of information from these workers over a two-year period starting before the plant closure. The men were aware of the impending redundancies. The data collected were extensive and included physiological measures (for example, blood pressure and urine samples), social psycho-logical data (for example, information about their ability to relax with people), and health data (for example, questionnaire measures of how well the person felt).

Examining changes in blood pressure, they found that there was what they called an 'anticipation' effect with BP rising when the men were still at work but aware of the impending close-down. The amount of the rise was related to the extent to which the men found the period particularly stressful. They also found that the BP of those men who quickly found re-employment began to drop rapidly, whereas the BP of those who experienced longer periods of unemployment tended to remain high. Again in terms of subjective stress the BP of those men who felt that the stress of the job loss experience had lasted a long time took longer to come down than those who felt that the period of stress had not lasted a long time. In terms of 'well-being' (measured on scales of depression, irritation, and self-esteem), the BP of those men who did not show much improvement tended to remain high whilst the BP of those who did report improvements in 'well-being' tended to return to normal more quickly. Finally, the chances of BP remaining high was also related to poor measures of adjustment and ego strength.

Similar findings for changes in serum uric acid and serum cholesterol levels were discovered, except that cholesterol levels showed no anticipation effect, and uric acid levels returned to normal more rapidly than BP levels when re-employment occurred.

In terms of reported illness and illness behaviour the subjects kept a health diary for various phases of fourteen days in which they recorded days when they 'did not feel as well as usual', and also days when they 'didn't carry on usual activities' due to illness or injury. The general findings were that those men who found the experience of unemployment to be more severe also indicated higher levels of days when they complained of illness, and higher levels of days of disability, and those who experienced more weeks of unemployment tended to show more days when they did not carry out their usual activities owing to illness or injury.

Turning to the psychological indices the findings were that the views the men had about their activities, their futures and their relations with other people, all appeared sensitive to both their subjective stress and their unemployed status. Measures were taken relating to: (a) keeping physically active and busy, using their skills and doing interesting things; (b) feeling secure about their future and in control of their fate; (c) feelings about getting ahead and receiving respect from others; and (d) being able to relax with people around them and confide in them regarding various problems. The findings were that in almost all of these areas the men were more dissatisfied and unhappy as they experienced the job loss and found difficulty in finding new work. Perhaps a more significant finding was that even after two years from the closing of the plants the men showed a much greater level of dissatisfaction than a control group. When one considers that the majority of the men had by this time found re-employment it would seem that 'in their perceptions of their future and of their life in general the men had been permanently and irreversibly affected by the plant closings and the subsequent experiences' (Kasl and Cobb 1971 : 104).

What is the significance of these findings? As the authors conclude in one of their papers (Kasl, Gore, and Cobb 1975) making definitive statements about the effects of *one* stressful life event is exceedingly difficult. Not having medical backgrounds ourselves, it would be presumptuous of us to comment except in laymen's terms on the effects of the variety of changes noted above. However, even laymen would feel confident in assuming that a cluster of changes such as those described would tend to lower resistance and increase the possibility of some form of pathological reaction. For example, high BP and high cholesterol levels are major predisposing factors for coronary heart diseases (heart attacks) and also cerebrovascular diseases (strokes) – two of the most common forms of death in Britain and America (see House 1974). Also findings on the incidence of peptic ulcer rates of various occupational groups suggest that the greater levels of responsibility and/or interpersonal tension predispose men to ulcers (see Susser 1967). Whilst not examined specifically in the studies by Kasl and Cobb, one might suggest that subjective feelings of responsibility (for example, for the family), would increase as the means of fulfilling that responsibility decreases (for example, less finance), and this could well connect with increases in interpersonal tensions in the family. Kahn and French (1970) report a set of findings showing that self-esteem in work decreases with decreasing status while occurrence of peptic ulcer rates rises as self-esteem declines. Virtually all studies of unemployed people show a decline in self-esteem connected with the loss of the status of employed person.

In a psycho-social study of worker reaction to job loss due to plant closure Strange (1977) gives brief case studies of six of the thirty subjects. The first describes a man who in addition to feeling continually fatigued had a diminished appetite and weight loss; the second had similar characteristics but in addition developed an ulcer after two months of unemployment. The third had an incipient ulcer and had also blacked out. There had been a marked increase in drinking. This increase in drinking was characteristic of the fourth case though here there had been an alcohol problem of long standing. Whilst in employment this problem had apparently been controlled but re-emerged with unemployment. Accompanying this problem was nervousness, restlessness, loss of interest in daily activities, difficulty in concentrating, diminished attention span, and tightness of the stomach. The fifth case was complicated by the fact that the subject had a pre-existing illness, but as Strange reports: 'an apparent withdrawal and cessation of former interests such as hunting and a rapid deep breathing and slurred speech apparent at interview are suggestive of considerable internal tension' (Strange 1978 : 419). The final case was characterized by the familiar difficulties in sleeping and also the development of an apparently serious ulcer, which during his period of unemployment got worse. The subject collapsed and was hospitalized for seventeen days.

There were others in the study who reacted to job loss with even greater severity, but in giving these six descriptions we are intending to give a more qualitative picture of the physical reactions than the essentially quantitative data presented in the Kasl and Cobb studies.

We shall now move on to examine what might be viewed as the ultimate reaction an individual can make to an existence that he or she finds intolerable – suicide.

SUICIDE AND UNEMPLOYMENT

Whilst extensive studies have been carried out examining theories, predisposing characteristics, and causes of suicide, few of these have concerned themselves with the relationship between suicide and unemployment *per se*. However, in an examination of the researches we find that unemployment appears time and again as one of the factors that seems to correlate with suicide. Once again, however, the nature of the relationship is difficult to define. Is the high incidence of unemployed persons committing suicide due to their unemployed status, or do factors that lead to suicide also make it difficult for them to sustain employment, or is it an interdependence of the two?

Looking at research carried out in the 1920s and 1930s we find numerous studies that show correlations between unemployment and suicides, and also between suicides and economic and business activity. Sainsbury (1955) reports that in America and Britain various studies found negative correlations between suicide rates and business conditions. His own analysis of the Registrar General's annual statistics showed there to be a rise in suicide during the depression of 1930–32. Sainsbury also found that in London the unemployed had a much higher suicide rate than the employed and that in about one-third of the unemployed suicides, unemployment was given as the principal cause. A more recent study by Sathyvathi (1977) of the relationship between unemployment and suicide in Bangalore found that of the 171 cases of unemployed suicides between 1967–73, 65 per cent had committed suicide either because of unemployment as the only reason or for reasons in addition to unemployment. Buglas and Horton (1974), comparing the characteristics of para-suicides (attempted suicides) over a three-year period, 1968–70, found that unemployment was a significant factor in the characteristics of repeaters as against non-repeaters. Finally, to redress the balance of the above findings, Walbran, MacMahon, and Bailey (1965) found no correlation between suicide rates and unemployment in Pennsylvania between 1954–61.

What are we to make of such findings? Durkheim (1933) argued that one factor which affected the suicide rate of a community was the extent to which individuals identified with the social groups that control and define their activities. As we have seen in previous chapters, not only is the unemployed person unable to identify with previous groups that were part and parcel of the sustenance of his or her identity, but the relationships with those groups he or she still remains part of (for example, the family), are often altered because of unemployment.

In addition to the above, sudden adversity which affects individuals is a commonly observed antecedent to suicide, and again as we have seen in many cases adversity is a common feature of unemployed people's existences. Also individuals who are made unemployed can often end up viewing their predicament as a reflection on themselves rather than as the result of outside forces. In one sense one would not expect 'role failure' in one area of a person's life to lead to suicide; the argument is, however, that in some cases the change from employment to unemployment may, because of changes in free time, contacts with others, etc. produce changes and conflicts in a variety of significant and central roles. Thus, there may be a cumulative effect which might in some individuals produce an intolerable situation. They might see suicide as the only way out. In terms of this perspective Gibbs and Martin (1964) report that status integration (based on occupational categories) is inversely related to suicide, and Breed (1963) concluded that the problem of downward mobility associated with unemployment and work-related difficulties increased the likelihood of suicide.

Again, the difficulty in all these studies is in establishing the significance of the various factors which are changed through employment. What we feel, however, is that the evidence from such a variety of studies would seem to suggest that unemployment is a factor which in some cases could well precipitate suicide. The number of cases reported in the media in 1980, giving unemployment as the main reason for suicide, adds support to such an assertion.

UNEMPLOYMENT AND MENTAL HEALTH

In a very real sense the whole of this book is an attempt to examine the mental health consequences of unemployment, and thus a specific section on the relationship might at first seem out of place.

Like the first section of this chapter evidence for a direct relationship between mental health and unemployment is scarce, in the sense of hard facts, and also problematic in terms of the nature of the relationship. Particularly problematic, when considering this area, is what is meant by mental health. The definition and measurement of mental illness is an issue which has plagued most researchers (see Sells 1969), and is one which we shall consider later in the chapter.

The work carried out by Jaco (1960) in his analysis of first-time psychiatric patients in Texas between 1951-52 is relevant in that he found that the unemployed (classified as those attempting to obtain employment at the time they became psychotic), had the highest adjusted incidence rates of psychosis, and that this held for 'both sexes, in each of the sub-cultural groups, for every type of mental disorder and for both public and private courses of psychiatric treatment.' He also found that whereas the unemployed made up 2.1 per cent of the population they accounted for 7.6 per cent of the psychotic group.

A more recent piece of research investigating the work histories of psychiatric patients (Schaffer 1976) found that the severity of psychiatric disorders and disturbances appeared to be related to the type and level of job opportunities available to the subjects, and that the findings of the study supported Wilson, Berry, and Miskimins' (1969) conclusion that there was an inverse relationship between the severity of maladjustment and vocational success. Wilson, Berry and Miskimins also found that 'vocationally successful patients had been hospitalised less than subjects considered to be vocational failures' (Schaffer 1976: 334).

Griffiths, Hodgson, and Hallam (1974), in attempting to assess the work prospects of psychiatric patients, found evidence to suggest that ratings of drive, self-confidence, and the patient's views of their disablement, were variables which differentiated those who were employed and those who were not employed at a follow up time averaging fifteen months from the initial assessment.

On the basis of all these findings it is not possible to separate the extent to which mental disorders are a factor which leads to unemployment, or whether unemployment causes mental disorders which then make re-employment more difficult. Clearly there are many patients with disorders unrelated to unemployment and for whom these disorders prevent or make it difficult to get work, but equally clearly, as we have shown in preceding chapters, unemployment does require a psychological adjustment which in some cases may contribute to mental disorders.

The findings of Morgan and Cheadle (1975) on the relationship between levels of unemployment and the resettlement of patients from psychiatric hospital provide an important reminder that an individual's rehabilitation is not simply a question of his or her own mental improvement, but is related to the availability of jobs in the community. They found that the ability to place patients in employment became progressively more difficult as unemployment rose above 2 per cent and suggest that placement would be practically impossible with unemployment at 6 per cent. They conclude that

> 'The prevailing levels of unemployment appear to us to determine within fairly narrow limits the disposal of a number of patients of otherwise uncertain prognosis. Given conditions of high employment they can live and work in the community and have no need of a hospital bed or sheltered work place. Given high unemployment social pressures will consign them to and keep them in hospital. Few will be able to leave unless sheltered work is available for them. Efforts to rehabilitate and resettle them in the community will not be viable unless through put is ensured by the same means.'
>
> (Morgan and Cheadle 1975:67)

The import of Morgan and Cheadle's findings does not depend on the nature of the relationship between unemployment and mental health, for, regardless of the cause of the mental disorder, if unemployment is at a high level then few patients are going to be rehabilitated into the community. What stems from these findings is the hidden costs both in financial, social and human terms, that arise as a consequence of high levels of unemployment. In financial and social terms it means that more hospital places are required. In human terms it means that the chances of resettlement, an essential element in the treatment of many disorders, is greatly reduced. Finally, if unemployment is a factor which increases the possibility of mental disorders, then in times of high unemployment not only is there a probability of an increase in the number of people suffering from some sort of mental illness, but the means by which these people may be treated are decreased.

So far our discussion of the mental health consequences of unemployment has been concerned with clinically defined cases. If we broaden our definition of mental health, then we can realize a whole range of new data that is relevant for understanding the relationship between mental health and unemployment. Two basic definitions that Margolis and Kroes (1974:139) give are: (1) the absence of mental illness, and (2) the optimum level of psychological functioning that an individual can sustain. Adapting the latter of these definitions we would say, for the purposes of the perspectives put forward in this book, that an individual is not in a mentally healthy state when his or her psychological functioning is such that his or her state of 'well-being' is impaired. Whilst realizing that such a definition is itself fraught with conceptual and operational difficulties, we nevertheless feel that it supplies a useful framework for considering the impact of unemployment. Adopting this broad definition we see that the vast majority of the cases quoted in this book come within the framework. In Daniel's (1974) extensive survey of the unemployed it was found that whilst the most common reason for being concerned at being out of work was financial, a majority also mentioned the psychological and social costs of unemployment. Boredom and inactivity was the most common complaint followed by depression and apathy. Thirdly, was the feeling of failure and uselessness and finally a few mentioned the social isolation and feeling of rejection from others because of their unemployed status.

Lee Rainwater, in a paper entitled 'Work, Well-being and Family Life', argues that a person's well-being is a function of the extent to which they are able to engage in 'validating activities':

'those activities that confirm an individual's sense of himself as a full and recognised member of society. . . . It is through engaging in activities that an individual achieves such a sense of concordance between what others consider him to be (social placement) and what he feels himself to be (personal identity) [and], . . . If he feels that there is much "dead time" in his life, much time in which there is "nothing to do", then his chances of achieving well-being are reduced.'

(Rainwater 1974:361–62)

Even a cursory glance at some of the case studies of the unemployed shows that the loss of the means for engaging in the 'validating activities' associated with work produces at least a reduction in well-being, and, more often than not, feelings of depression, anxiety, and hopelessness. The extent to which such reactions lead to an individual being medically defined as mentally ill, or whether individuals are able to cope with such reactions without recourse to the medical practitioners is not known. What is known is that such reactions do occur frequently, and must be seen in our view as a powerful psychological consequence of an individual being made unemployed.

As we stated at the beginning of this chapter we did not feel it possible, given the nature of the relationship between an event and the possible health consequences, and also because of the lack of research in the area, to come to any definite conclusions. In describing the ISR model as a framework within which to view the relationship, we attempted to show the complexity of establishing such a relationship, and thus to show why definite conclusions would be difficult to establish.

Nevertheless, when the evidence from the variety of diverse researches and case studies described in this book is grouped together, it does form a consistent picture. This picture, admittedly in the form of a pastiche, suggests that for the majority of people, unemployment produces a stress reaction which for many results in a strain on their physical and mental functioning. The particular outcome of such strain varies with the individual and his or her circumstances, but, in the final analysis, what we have shown is that *some* form of pathological response is a possible outcome for many people who become unemployed.

6 Interaction and identity strain for the unemployed

> 'The Value or Worth of a man, is as of all other things his Price; that is to say, so much as would be given for the use of his Power; and therefore, is not absolute; but a thing dependent on the need and judgement of another. . . . And as in other things so in men, not the seller, but the buyer determines the Price. For let a man (as most men do) rate themselves as the highest value they can; yet their true value is no more than it is esteemed by others.'
>
> THOMAS HOBBES, *Leviathan*, 1651

Throughout what has been written in previous chapters there has been an implicit assumption that the effects of unemployment are connected with the view the individual has of him- or herself, and the way in which this is affected by the loss of the means by which this view is maintained. As stated in the introduction, there still prevails some of the assumptions of a nineteenth-century Poor Law perspective on unemployment in which economic factors may be disregarded and the unemployed may feel that their situation is attributable to their own personal failings and faults.

However, what the prevailing perspective is, is less important than what the unemployed perceive it to be, because it is their perception, whether realistic or not, which helps to maintain their self-image. A major factor throughout the researches that we have examined, and mentioned frequently in our own interviews, is the references made by the unemployed to how they think others are viewing them. As one person said to us, 'You begin to think other people think you're lazy.' This feeling that others are judging them was a common finding of research carried out in the 1930s. Bakke quotes one man as saying:

> 'I know that things are slack, but I've always said that a good man could get a job even in a slack time. That's not so and the man who says so is a liar. . . . I feel when I walk down the

streets here that all my old mates are looking at me and saying, "Wonder what's wrong with 'A'? He never used to be away from work so long." Even my family is beginning to think I'm not trying. So I can't talk much with them any more.'

(Bakke 1933:65)

This view that others might judge them, or concern with the way others see them, is also reflected in the secrecy some of the unemployed adopt in order to 'manage' how others view him. As Briar says:

'The workers did not always tell their neighbours that they were jobless. This was not the depression where everyone was in a similar situation and relied on neighbours for help, this was only a "recession" and the neighbours did not need to know.'

(Briar 1977:56)

This notion of 'managing' how others view us, is a central feature of a symbolic interactionist perspective in which a person's self or self-image, 'a set of attitudes, beliefs and opinions held by a person about himself', is 'actually embedded in a set of social relationships that give it stability and continuity' (Faunce 1968:93). It seems to us that not only is this perspective useful in helping to understand the importance of work and the consequent effect this has on the type and nature of social relationships developed whilst at work, and thus on the type and nature of the self-image, but also, because of the loss of some of the relationships and the change in meaning assigned to still existent relationships, it helps to understand the 'identity strain' brought about by unemployment. As Hopson and Adams state, 'Identity strain exists when an individual feels unable to implement his self image in social roles he perceives to be important' (Hopson and Adams 1976:8).

A symbolic interactionist view of self contains the notion that not only do individuals have an image of themselves, but that this image is evaluated in terms of social categories, definitions and positions, and secondly, that this evaluation is based on, and can only ultimately survive within, certain sets of relationships.

Thus the self from a symbolic interactionist perspective is not seen as a fixed entity, but rather as something which is susceptible to change over time, as the social relationships which are a central part of its affirmation change. As most people have a fairly fixed set of social relationships in their family, friends, and work, there develops over time a residual core which, although socially derived, is less susceptible to change. It is just this residual core which is threatened when unemployment changes those relationships.

In so far as a person evaluates him- or herself, he or she does so through taking the role of the other, and applies the others categories, definitions and positions to the self. As Mead put it, 'But it is . . . when he not only hears himself, talks and replies to himself as truly as the other person replies to him, that we have behaviour in which individuals become objects to themselves' (Mead 1934:147). Thus, a man may see himself as a father, a husband, a breadwinner, a worker, etc., but further than that he sees himself as a particular type of father, husband, etc. For example, he is the father who, through his position as breadwinner, is accorded status in the family; he is the provider not only of the bread but the bike as well; the owner of the car as well as the free time, which is legitimized within the family because of the time he has spent at work. All these evaluations are developed and reaffirmed in the ongoing interactions of his daily existence. As Stone and Schlamp suggest:

'All these elements are tied together in the worker's conception of himself as breadwinner. The breadwinner role is significant first because of the necessity for cash income to maintain a livelihood within an industrial order. Beyond this level of necessity, the breadwinner role functions in the life of the worker to link him to the Protestant Ethic of the dominant society, at the same time that it is significant for his self-definition as a man. His male ego – his conception of himself as a man – is both experienced and reinforced by working, by income, and by participation in the microculture and informal relationships on the job.'   (Stone and Schlamp 1971:227)

The locations in which the individual exists, the family, the workplace, etc., are thus structured in such a way as to bestow and maintain a particular form of self-image, and whilst minor alterations in these structures will affect and change the self-image the locations remain, and the residual core may remain intact or subject to only minor change.

Whilst the various locations may differ in the significance they have for the individual, both in terms of the centrality of a location for supplying the means for the development and affirmation of a self-image, and in the meanings attached to activities in the location, for the majority, the location of work is not only highly significant in terms of time, but also in terms of status. The notion of status in this context is not in terms of the 'high' status of a judge or doctor, and the 'low' status of a road sweeper or dustman, though these status differentials may be important and significant for individuals, rather the significance of work is in the status of a person who actually earns his or her *own* living, that is, the status of 'worker'. As Jahoda puts it:

'Employment also provides some definition of one's position in society, status and identity. Of course people may resent the particular status accorded to their particular job and try to change it. But this is different from having no defined position. The unemployed suffer not only from the absence of status but even more from an undermining of their sense of personal identity.'   (Jahoda 1979:313)

This notion of status and its relationship with personal identity is, we believe, fundamental in any understanding of the psychology of unemployment. What follows from the loss of status of being a working person is a threat to the integrity of the person's self-image. Implicit in this notion of 'the integrity of the self-image' is the view of the individual at the centre of his or her conceptual world in which it is the individual who decides and chooses how he or she is going to be seen by others and ultimately by his- or herself. Of course, these decisions are made within the structures laid down by the particular social system in which the individual exists, but the norms of the work ethic are so powerfully embedded within this structure that it is for most people an unquestioned facet of their existence.

Thus, what we have is the individual's personal identity being developed, managed, and affirmed through the status of working person. When this status is removed it is not simply a question of the individual who loses the status of a working person, but more importantly he or she loses the means by which the integrity of the self-image is maintained. It is in this sense, then, that the individual loses some of the control over how he or she is to be seen.

As Strange says of his sample:

'Whereas at the plant they were used to being distinctive personalities with known attributes and built up credits, now

they became in a sense objectified – a set of impersonal data on an application form, a process which seemed antithetical to the life they had led, which further highlighted their vulnerabilities.'
(Strange 1978:422)

An additional point with respect to this notion of control over how a person is seen and how a person sees himself, relates to the unemployed person's new 'status' as welfare dependent. As Stone and Schlamp point out:

'Welfare status has the unique quality in that the state accepts obligation for the individual only because of his inability to hold any other status from which he can claim rights. . . .

[Thus] The welfare person, by social definition, is an individual whose status is not defined by reciprocity. There is nothing that the welfare person does, by virtue of his status that matches the responsibility assumed by the state. . . . There is nothing that the welfare client can do within the context of his dependent condition that merits respect. His only solution to this lack of respect is to remove himself from it. If this is not possible then some form of adaptation must take place leading either to redefinition of self and the adoption of alternative values, or to some individual form of escape from his situation or to the acceptance of defeat.'
(Stone and Schlamp 1971:241)

Thus the position of the unemployed is not simply the 'absence of status', but rather the absence of a status through which they realize themselves, coupled with the imposition of a status of welfare dependent. The move, then, is from a position of control and responsibility to one of, in many cases, total dependency.

An analogy may help to bring out this point. Work is a man (or woman's) right arm. Whilst he has it he may be more or less conscious of it; it may be more or less significant for him (for example, an arthritic will be more conscious of his arm, a darts player's arm will be more significant to him). The point, however, is that if the individual loses his right arm, he loses the means by which he has been able to engage in a whole range of activities which are central to him and he is seen by others as less than a whole person. The ultimate is that the right arm is no longer able to scratch the left arm, which must be related to only through some external source, and also he is no longer able to shake hands in the normal way, that is, the loss of the arm means the loss of a means by which he relates both to himself and others.

The import of this analogy is that whilst at work many may not be conscious of the function work serves as an identity bestowing structural location, the loss of work, however, brings out the importance of this function. What follows from this, then, is that a particular social status does not involve a single isolated role, but entails a variety of associated roles which may affect outside the particular location which is central in bestowing the status. Thus in Merton's terminology, the status of work entails a 'role-set by which I mean that complement of role relationships which persons have by virtue of occupying a particular social status' (Merton 1968:209). It is in this sense that the loss of work involves more than the loss of a particular role, it spills over to threaten a whole complement of role relationships which through overlap with other role sets may encompass the majority of an individual's life space.

The relationship between a symbolic interactionist analysis of the effects of unemployment and the analyses given in Chapters 2 and 3 is one of complementarity rather than conflict. Thus, the forces in Lewin's model, which we argued in the minimization stage an individual will attempt to maintain, are actually manifest in and subject to change by the interactions in which individuals engage in their daily lives. It is by 'managing' these interactions in particular ways that individuals try to develop and maintain both the view they have of themselves, and the view that others have of them. In adopting this perspective of symbolic inter-actionism, in which it is assumed that not only are the everyday interactions in which an individual engages important for main-taining and developing a self-image, but also that the individual tries to 'manage' these interactions in order to *promote* a particular self-image, we think it is possible to come to a clearer under-standing of the behaviours which individuals adopt.

The remainder of this chapter, then, will be concerned to examine a variety of scenarios in which unemployed people become involved. The analysis of these scenarios will be based on a perspective in which the unemployed individuals are attempting to 'manage' a self-image which they believe is threatened by their present situation.

In what ways, therefore, does this 'managing' manifest itself?

SECRECY AND DISTANCING

One of the features of the unemployed which Briar (1977) found in her sample was a strong desire for secrecy. This can be seen as a deliberate strategy to preserve their status as employed persons, and 'to protect themselves from being labelled as failures and from further degradation' (Briar 1977:56). As one worker, who did not tell his wife for two weeks that he had been made unemployed, explained, 'she [the wife] was the last to know of those who should have known' (Briar 1977:56). This strategy of preserving secrecy which may be seen as an attempt to maintain in the eyes of others the status of employed person can also be seen as an attempt to distance themselves from the prescribed status of unemployed 'welfare dependent', a label which they feel others could attach to them, were they to know of their true situation.

This idea of 'distancing' and 'secrecy' was brought home powerfully to one of us when working on a welfare rights stall, giving information on the availability of welfare benefits. One strategy, which many of the people who came to the stall adopted, was to make clear that their enquiry was not for themselves but for some relative or friend. They were, they said, just passing, and on seeing the stall thought they would see if there was any information which would be useful for their friend. In the process of discussing the circumstances of their friend and their friend's entitlements two factors would often emerge. Firstly, these people had a considerable amount of knowledge and information about their 'friends'' predicament, for example, how much rent they paid, whether they had other sources of income, the ages of their children, etc., and secondly, in some cases they would 'slip up' in their 'managing' and talk in the first person. For example, instead of saying, 'They don't have any savings,' they would say, 'We don't have any savings.' It became obvious in these cases that these people were actually talking about themselves rather than another person.

The second strategy of 'distancing' also occurred quite frequently. In this scenario the person starts by explaining that they are not like 'those lazy scroungers who haven't done a day's work in their lives,' and 'it's ridiculous, something ought to be done about them'. Then, having spent this time negotiating their own status as being different from the status they perceived to be attached to a person in this situation, they proceeded to make their enquiry as to their entitlements. In talking to some of the people who adopt this second strategy one is often struck by the venomous way in which they castigate others who are in a similar predicament to themselves. If one perceives what is going on in terms of 'distancing' one becomes aware of the very real threat that these people feel of being seen in a way that they feel unemployed people are seen.

TWO CASE STUDIES

We shall now consider two case studies which we believe bring out the complexity of the process of 'managing' a self-image when unemployed.

Adopting a dramaturgical approach, it seems to us that one can differentiate between those cases where the stage is set and the lines of the 'others' already written, and those cases where the individuals set the stage themselves and negotiate the parts and the lines of both themselves and the others. This differentiation is for analytical purposes only and empirically there is much overlapping in the two scenarios. The following is an account of the first of these two scenarios, and, whilst it is an outline of an actual case, it does contain many facets which are frequently mentioned in the researches and in our interviews with unemployed people.

Case 1: claiming welfare benefits

This case concerns an unemployed general labourer who had been out of work for fifteen months. The information contained here is based on detailed notes taken by a member of the Leeds Poverty Action Group who accompanied the claimant to his local Department of Health and Social Security Office to help him claim what he thought was a discrepancy in his benefit. Whilst the fact that someone was with him will have affected the situation, observations of other interactions in DHSS offices, comments made to us by other claimants, and comments made by officials of the DHSS, convince us that the situation described here is not atypical. In fact, a recently leaked internal report from the DHSS about the working of DHSS offices gives substance to much of the scenario put forward here (see Moore 1980).

For example, the author of the report states,

'concern to prevent abuse was probably the single most significant influence on staff's attitudes to and dealings with
claimants, [and] . . .

Because there was a possibility of abuse in so many cases,
an air of suspicion commonly underlay interviews, and was
hard to conceal. Questioning a claimant with one eye on his
welfare needs, and the other on the possibility of fraud was an
impossible schizophrenic role. And with some staff, the
suspicious eye became much the sharper of the two.'

(Moore 1980:68)

The case. The first thing that struck you after getting used to
the drab and dingy decor of the waiting area in the DHSS office
was the fact that the chairs were screwed to the floor. The second
was the 'No Smoking' sign and the cigarette ends which littered
the floor and thirdly, was the iron grills in the cubicles which
separated the unemployed from the officials who would deal with
their cases. This then is the scenery within which the play was to
be acted. Mr X had gone to the reception counter and had been
told that he should sit down and that his name would be called,
'when it's your turn to be dealt with'. He waited for forty minutes
before he was called to cubicle six.

Official:	'What appears to be the problem Mr X?'
Mr X:	'I've checked through what I'm due and I'm getting four pound short.'
Official:	'Yes, well we checked this through after you came last time and what you've forgotten to take into account is the deduction of four pounds a week maintenance that your wife gets for her first child by her former husband.'
Mr X:	'But I told them two weeks ago that he doesn't send it any more, she hasn't had anything for months.'
Official:	'Have you tried to contact him and get the money?'
Mr X:	'I told them before that he's moved and we don't know where he is.'
Official:	'Does he come and see the child?'
Mr X:	'No, he hasn't been for months.'
Official:	'Do you have any idea where he may have gone?'
Mr X:	'No, I don't.'

Official: 'Well, why didn't you come and see us straight away
            when he stopped paying maintenance?'
Mr X: 'Sometimes he wouldn't pay for a few weeks then
            when he'd got some money he'd come round and
            see the kid and give her some money. We thought
            he might come.'
Official: 'Do you think that's what's happened this time?'
Mr X: 'What?'
Official: 'Do you think he might come round and give her
            some money when he gets some?'
Mr X: 'I don't know.'
Official: 'I'll have to go and see someone about this, if you'll
            just take your seat I'll call you when we've decided
            what to do.'

Mr X returned to his seat for twenty minutes.

Official: 'Mr X to cubicle eight'.
Official: 'Well, what we've decided to do is to pay the four
            pounds maintenance for the last two weeks, but if
            your wife's former husband pays her any money,
            you'll have to tell us and we'll deduct it from your
            weekly benefit. When you see him you'll have to get
            him to pay the maintenance because it's his duty to
            support the child, not ours.'
Mr X: 'I've told you, we haven't seen him for months.'
Official: 'Well, anyway, we'll send you a giro for the last two
            weeks.'

Outside the office.

Observer: 'Well, you've got the money.'
Mr X: 'That bastard was calling me a liar. You'd think it
            was his bloody money he was giving out. Honestly,
            she hasn't seen him for months.'

Analysis.   The first point that needs to be made in relation to the
structural parameters of the interaction is that the DHSS is a
bureaucracy in which much of Merton's (1940) criticisms seem to
apply. In response to a fairly substantial media coverage of cases
of abuse (see Nutman 1977; Lythgoe, 1979), the demand for
control from the top hierarchy has increased, with the con-

sequent increase in the rigidity of behaviour and tightening of rules predicted by Merton. This then affects the approach to and perspective on the client that the official brings to the interaction. As Berger and Luckman say, 'The reality of everyday life contains typificatory schemes in terms of which others are apprehended and "dealt with" in face to face encounters' (Berger and Luckman 1967:45). Thus it is not simply the case that the official's 'typificatory schemes' are altered in the light of the other's behaviour, but also that the 'typificatory schemes' are altered by the structure and rules of the organization which play an important part in defining the way in which the official relates to the client.

Thus, in this particular case, the 'typificatory scheme' that the official brings to the interaction is based on the facts that Mr X is available for work, but has been unemployed for fifteen months, and he is claiming for a discrepancy in his benefit which is easily open to abuse, that is, it is very difficult for the DHSS to check whether the former husband is or is not paying maintenance. Given this perspective, clearly the official's role required that he establish as far as possible whether the case was legitimate. The important part of the analysis, which is relevant to our purpose, is how did the scenario appear to the unemployed person. One of the difficulties of a symbolic interactionist analysis is that the observer tends to impose meanings on the interaction from his own frame of reference, and this may not coincide with the framework from which the individual perceives the situation. None the less, it is possible to pick up clues and cues from the interaction, which give some guide to the analyst that he is on the right lines.

Firstly, Mr X asked the observer if he thought the cubicles were like the visiting cubicles in prisons, and secondly, when he offered the observer a cigarette and the observer pointed out that there was a 'No Smoking' sign his response was, 'They can't keep you waiting this long, and not expect you to smoke.' Thus, whilst he may not have been viewing the environment in the same way as the observer, it was something that he was conscious of. The second point is that a common feature of most visits to social security offices is that the clients are kept waiting for long periods. This is, in most cases, due to lack of resources (staff to deal with the cases), but as Schwarz comments, the psychological aspects of delay, which affect, regardless of the reasons for the delay, serve to define the relationship between the parties in the interaction:

> 'The person who is delayed is not merely in a condition of objective dependence and subordination; because his only duty is to attend the call of the server the waiter feels dependent and subordinate. To be kept waiting – especially to be kept waiting an unusually long time – is to be the subject of an assertion that one's own time (and therefore one's social worth), is less valuable than the time and the worth of the one who imposes the wait. . . . Of course, waiting does not create the sense of subordination but only accentuates an initial inferiority, which is often presupposed by the fact that one is waiting in the first place. It needs to be said that this sentiment has its parallel on the other side of the relationship for the server calls out in himself the response that he elicits in the ones he keeps waiting, which enables him not only to be conscious of his own power – to see himself from the point of view of his clients – but also to feel within himself the independent power that he extracts from those who wait for him.'
>
> (Schwarz 1974 : 856)

Mr X's reaction to the delay was to get increasingly fidgety and frustrated. In terms of the actual interaction Mr X was fidgeting and towards the end was gripping his hands together under the table, and, as the interview continued, his voice increased in intensity. In discussing what had happened, he later said that he was getting more and more angry 'with the bastard' but was trying not to lose his temper, ''Cos we had to have the money.' This is, in a sense, an example of a 'situational adjustment' which Becker expands as follows:

> 'The person as he moves in and out of a variety of social situations, learns the requirements of continuing in each situation and of success in it. If he has a strong desire to continue, the ability to assess accurately what is required, and can deliver the required performance, the individual turns himself into the kind of person the situation demands.'
>
> (Becker 1964 : 44)

Thus Mr X was 'managing' his interaction in a way he perceived to be most effective for bringing about his desired goal, but whilst it was *he* who was 'managing' this had to be done within a framework almost entirely defined by the other and the situation. The meanings through which Mr X interpreted the interaction were in terms of the official viewing him as a liar, as someone who was trying to 'fiddle' the system, and his reaction to that interpretation was to get angry.

The observer spent some time with Mr X after the interview trying to calm him down, and attempting to give him an 'appropriate' way of looking at what had happened in order that he should feel that what had occurred was not really a reflection on himself, but was rather the inevitable consequence of a bureaucratic system. In other words the observer was attempting to 'cool the mark out'. 'For the mark, cooling represents a process of adjustment to an impossible situation – a situation arising from having defined himself in a way that the social facts have come to contradict' (Goffman 1952:456). Because of his objective circumstances Mr X had had to enter an environment which he perceived as threatening and frustrating, and engage in an interaction which, because of his need for money, he felt required him passively to accept a definition of himself which was at variance with the way he defined himself. Given this perception of the situation, his ability to control how he should be seen was denied him, and if we are right in what we said earlier about the notion of control over an individual's environment (see Chapter 3), he was thus denied the opportunity of reaffirming his identity and self-image.

The account and analysis given of this particular interaction is an attempt to probe in a more meaningful way these sorts of enforced situations and the meanings these situations have for the unemployed in terms of their self-image and self-respect.

Case 2: meeting people

A common feature of nearly all the research studies into the effects of unemployment has been the feeling held by the unemployed that people view them or treat them differently because of their changed status. For example Briar (1977) reports that at least half her sample felt that others had treated them differently. The reality here, that is whether there is evidence that people change their behaviour in relation to a person because of his or her changed status, is less important than the fact that the unemployed perceive this change to have taken place. It is, after all, on the basis of their perceptions that people form views and opinions of others and of themselves, whether or not these perceptions are realistic or not.

As pointed out earlier in this chapter, and in Chapter 4, a person's occupational status is a significant feature of what that person is. Knowledge of the occupational status of a person not only gives one cues as to how to relate to him or her, but often provides cues as to the content of the interaction.

A person who has previously held an occupational status of whatever type has had experience (though not necessarily consciousness), of the often subtle ways in which such a status affects interactions with others. However, with the status of unemployment there comes the possibility of being defined as one of a group of people to whom particular and often more negative stereotypes are seen to apply. It is within this framework of others viewing them according to these stereotypes that the unemployed often engage in interactions. The following case attempts to show one of the many possible ways that unemployed people try to show that such stereotypical views do not apply to them.

The situation is a fairly common one in which a friend of a member of a social group is introduced to that group. The social group is made up of four people of varying occupational statuses and the friend is a person who has been unemployed for three months. The setting is a local public house where the group meet regularly for a drink and conversation.

The scenario is essentially of the second of the types mentioned earlier, viz: a situation in which the individual sets the stage and negotiates the parts and the lines for both himself and the others. It is also a scene in which an outsider has to negotiate his image within an already cohesive group.

The pertinent points in the interaction occurred when the people in the group got round to asking the friend what he did for a living. There followed a lengthy explanation of how up until recently he had been a junior executive, but had been dissatisfied with the way the firm had been run and in particular with the way they had treated their employees. He had therefore resigned. From this point on his status as an unemployed person, which was now public knowledge, seemed to become quite a central feature of his interactions with members of the group. He actually referred to himself as unemployed five times in the hour, though at each stage it was not relevant to the conversation. An interesting feature of this was that it was he who raised his status and not the others in the group, nor did it appear significant for them except in so far as he kept 'putting it on the agenda'. For example when it was his turn to buy the drinks he said, 'Drink up, have one on the unemployed,' and at another stage when talking about cars he said, 'We unemployed can't afford to run big cars.' These statements were made in a jovial manner and were accepted within the framework of someone having a 'dig' at himself, though not to be taken as a reflection of how the person viewed himself. In reflecting on what had occurred the observer attempted to analyse the interactions in terms of the negotiation of a particular self-image. He fed back his conclusions to his friend, who whilst using slightly different terminology and categories, accepted the analysis as a fair reflection of what had been going on.

Analysis. The main conclusions, then, were that the friend did not like the status of being unemployed, and thought that others viewed him less favourably because he was unemployed. He had, therefore, attempted to 'manage' the interaction in such a way that he was able to negotiate an image of himself such that whilst he held the objective status of unemployed person, his attitude to it as a reflection of self was that the status was temporary, and because of his reasons for leaving employment, a legitimate aberration. Thus his negotiation was an attempt to 'save face'. 'The phrase "to save face" appears to refer to the process by which the person sustains an impression for others that he has not lost face' (Goffman 1955:215). He was thus saying that whilst unemployment for many entails a 'loss of face', 'in my case, because it was I who made myself unemployed for what I perceive to be legitimate and, in fact, moral reasons, and because I am prepared to wear my unemployment like a badge for all to see, then you can see that unemployment for me is something I am in control of.' By actually taking charge of the conceptions and definitions by which others are to view him he is 'exerting leverage on others that allows him to maintain his conceptions of himself to some degree, as long as he can avoid tripping himself up through his own performance, people are obliged to give him the benefit of the doubt' (McCall and Simmons 1966:146). In this case, because the interaction was of a short duration, he was able to avoid 'tripping himself up', but the feeling of the observer who knew the group was that had he continued to emphasize his unemployment – as a status to be denied – then there may have been the possibility that the others might have started to view this on the lines of, 'The lady doth protest too much, methinks' (*Hamlet*, Act 3, Scene 2).

Another facet of the interaction which fits the analysis put forward above, is the fact that he made the sort of statements that he felt others might make against him as an unemployed person. Thus implicit in one of his statements, again made in a jovial manner, was the awareness that he was living off their taxes. This is not self-denigration, but rather by bringing the issue into the open he is preventing them from using it to define or criticize him, and secondly, by presenting it in a joking manner, he is showing that he does not see this as a serious criticism.

It is through this mechanism of 'getting the boot in to oneself' first, and showing that it does not hurt, that he shows to others that they will not pain him if they kick him in the same spot, and, therefore, it is not worth their while trying.

SUMMARY

What we have attempted to show in this chapter, by giving concrete examples of not untypical scenarios, is how unemployed people may be forced to 'manage' their interactions with others. In some cases this 'managing' may require that the unemployed do not defend themselves against unacceptable definitions which others may attempt to impose on them, whilst in other cases the 'managing' may involve intricate manoeuvres in order that a defence may be prepared against the imposition by others of possibly unacceptable definitions.

Symbolic interactionism, which lies behind much of the analysis presented here, is not a theory in the sense that hypotheses follow from it, rather it is an approach using a variety of interlocking concepts to help to understand and describe a variety of sociological and social-psychological phenomena. The focus in this chapter by concentrating on case studies from a symbolic interactionist perspective, has been to show how individuals may attempt to cope with and manage some aspects of their social environments.

In terms of the connection between this form of analysis and that put forward in previous chapters one could ask, in the case of the interaction with the DHSS official, 'How many times can individuals perform an acceptance of others' perceptions of themselves, before it starts to affect their own perceptions of themselves?', and in the second case, 'How long can people manage the perceptions others might have of them before either tripping themselves up or others tripping them up?'

7   Search behaviour

'There is no failure except in no longer trying.'
ELBERT HUBBARD, *The Note Book*, 1927

Loss of work can be experienced in a variety of ways. It can occur suddenly. The individual may be informed that the plant is to close down immediately and the loss of his or her job will be irrevocable. Alternatively, workers may live for months not knowing whether or not their jobs are safe and, even if they are eventually laid-off, they may not be certain whether the loss of work is irrevocable or just an unwelcome interruption to their career. Indeed, sometimes people may be recalled only to be made redundant once again at some later stage.

It is possible to identify two stages in the process of becoming unemployed. The first stage is a period during which the need for lay-offs becomes apparent to the employing organization and a redundancy programme is planned. Trade union officials may be involved in this process but usually great care is taken to maintain secrecy. The second stage is the period during which redundancies are announced and the people who are to lose their jobs are identified. One reason for secrecy in the first phase is the fear of what knowledge of the lay-offs could do to worker morale and performance. Hartley and Cooper (1978) indicate, however, that many of these fears may not be grounded in reality. None the less, this phase is still one which is shrouded in secrecy.

If the attempts to keep this early planning phase secret are successful then those people who are the targets for possible redundancy will not experience long periods of uncertainty and anxiety. Frequently, however, such secrecy is not maintained. Employees observe what is happening to people in other organizations throughout their industry and begin to wonder if the same thing might happen to them. They become anxious and sensitive to anything which threatens their security. In this climate rumours flourish and can be started in many different ways. Two people working for the same organization told us they knew 'something was in the offing' because one morning the cleaners found that certain offices in the personnel department were locked. This discovery rekindled memories of a similar incident ten years earlier which had been followed by an announcement of redundancies. Increased stock levels, economy drives or an unusually harassed management team can provide the source of rumours which may or may not accurately reflect or predict the onset of redundancies. At this stage, however, it is the very existence of the rumours rather than their accuracy which creates the uncertainty and anxiety. This uncertainty will continue, even when management has confirmed that some redundancies may be inevitable. People will want to know precisely who will be affected and when the lay-offs are likely to occur.

Uncertainty about the future creates problems for many people, not only those who will eventually lose their jobs. The greater the uncertainty the more the dilemmas that people have to face. A conversation we had with a worried housewife illustrated one such dilemma. She told us how her husband had lost weight and aged through worrying about whether or not he should change jobs. He had worked for the same organization all his life, as had his father before him. The cause of the dilemma had been a rumour, which management would neither confirm nor deny, that his firm might be forced to close down. In this kind of situation it is not always easy for an individual to decide whether to embark on a job search, accept the offer of alternative employment, or stay where he is in the hope that even if others are laid-off he will be allowed to retain his job. If the individual is tempted by job openings elsewhere he will have to weigh the pros and cons of resigning his present position now or waiting until he is made redundant. To resign, particularly for the long-serving employee, may mean forfeiting generous severance pay. In some circumstances this may be a very high cost for a very small benefit. The new job may not turn out to be much more secure than the present one and, if the new employer is faced with the need to shed workers, he may adopt a policy of 'last in, first out'. In these circumstances the individual will find himself made redundant after all but without the cushion of severance pay. The situation may be equally complicated if he decided to stay on in his present job. In due course his original fear of redundancy may be realized and he may discover, when he is eventually forced to search for alternative employment, that the job openings that were previously available no longer exist. Deciding whether, or when, to seek alternative work is only one of the many dilemmas created by the fear of possible redundancy. A young married couple we talked to were afraid of starting a family because they felt that the wife had a more secure job than the husband. Others could not decide whether to move house or change cars.

In an uncertain situation many people are inclined to regard the future pessimistically, to fear the worst and to act defensively. People we have spoken to who feared redundancy but who were retained by their employer when some of their colleagues were laid-off reported a feeling of reprieve. 'The fear was always there. It was like living under a shadow.' A husband and wife we interviewed said, 'We knew we were irritable at home, but it wasn't until it was all over that we realized what it had really been like. It must have been rough on the kids.' Unfortunately sometimes such reprieves are short lived. A person not affected by the first round of redundancies may find that his or her job is axed in a second round.

Not only is loss of work associated with different degrees of uncertainty, but also with differences in the period between the announcement of planned redundancies and the actual lay-off. Many organizations find themselves unable to give much notice because they are faced with a sudden and unanticipated deterioration in their trading position. Others are in a position to give considerable notice but fear that this could adversely affect morale and performance and could lead to the gradual erosion of key workers. Some firms, on the other hand, feel that as a matter of principle, every effort should be made to provide employees with as much notice as possible (see the example of British Steel in Chapter 8). There may be some relationship between the period of notice and the individual's ability to secure continuity of employment. Many of the people we talked to expressed the belief that it was easier for an employed person to change jobs than it was for unemployed persons to regain employment. We have not attempted to test this belief but some of the unemployed we encountered wished that they had been given longer notice so that they could have had more time to seek alternative work whilst still employed.

Those faced with the prospect of immediate redundancy may find themselves precipitated into a crisis situation whereas those who are given more lead time may have the opportunity to plan and can, if they wish, initiate and manage a process of personal change in preparation for their redundancy. Studies of bereavement have identified a process of anticipatory grieving (see Fulton and Fulton 1972) in which those close to someone dying rehearse the loss of the loved one and attempt to adjust to the various consequences of the loss. Similarly, the person under notice of redundancy and those close to him or her may rehearse an attempt to adjust to the impending change. They may therefore experience much of the shock, denial and depression associated with unemployment whilst still at work and may, at least in part, adjust to the prospect of redundancy before actually being laid-off. None the less, it is impossible to predict accurately the outcome of this process of anticipatory adjustment. Some may refuse to acknowledge that it will actually happen to them or that redundancy will mean a permanent and irrevocable break with their current employer.

Beliefs about call-back can, as noted in previous chapters, have an important influence on a person's job search behaviour. Those who believe that they are only being laid off temporarily 'until things improve' may be disinclined to seek out alternative jobs elsewhere, reluctant to embark on a programme of retraining or engage in other activities which may require them to modify the assumptions which they make about themselves in relation to the world of work. Consequently the individual who has been employed by an organization that only started laying people off after making extensive use of short-time working arrangements and which announced that people will be recalled as soon as the work is available may view his or her situation very differently from the individual who is unemployed because his or her old firm has closed down and gone out of business.

Where the status passage from employment to unemployment is shrouded in uncertainty, where the individual is given little lead time to adjust to the impending change and where there is little data upon which to develop realistic expectancies about call-back, then the individual is likely to experience more difficulty managing the transition. These difficulties may well be reflected in subsequent job search behaviour.

FUNCTIONS OF THE JOB HUNT

Maintenance

Unemployment, with very few exceptions, involves a transition which is neither desired nor sought. As we noted in Chapter 4, the majority of people appear to view it as a loss both in terms of attachment and detachment, and as we suggested in Chapter 3 they frequently behave in ways that reflect a reluctance to let go of the status of employed worker. This behaviour may well be evidenced in the individual's approach to the job hunt. For example, one of the commonly reported attachment losses associated with unemployment is the gain in free time. One way of filling this time is by engaging in the search for alternative sources of employment. Not only can this search be time consuming, but it may also require the individual to be relatively active. A frequently reported detachment-loss is the absence of structured activity, which the job hunt, along with gardening, decorating, and the like, can replace, at least in the short term. Another detachment-loss associated with unemployment is the loss of a sense of purpose. Again the job hunt can fill this void. It provides a focus for purposeful behaviour which is also seen as a worthy endeavour by those around him or her – the family, friends, and society at large. One important function of the job hunt then is maintenance. By substituting alternative sources of reinforcement for many of those normally derived from work, the individual is able to maintain some of his or her self-respect and sense of well-being.

Searching for that which was lost

As the term 'job hunt' implies, it is a form of search behaviour. Almost every transition is associated with some kind of searching. This is clearly illustrated by Parkes (1972) who identified four components of search behaviour in the newly bereaved:

(1) *Pining and a preoccupation with thoughts of the deceased person.* These thoughts tended to be painful because they were associated with a persistent wish for the person who was gone. The widows in Parkes' study tended to go over in their minds events of the past in which their husbands had taken part, and experienced extremely clear memories of the dead

person, not only his face, but also his voice and even his touch. Some also experienced haunting memories of the final illness or death. As we shall see, similar preoccupations with work can be observed among the unemployed.

(2) *Direction of attention towards places and objects associated with the lost person.* Many of the widows described feelings of being drawn towards places that they associated with their dead spouse and most of them treasured possessions that had previously belonged to him. However, some of the widows reported that old haunts and intimate articles could evoke such intense pining that they tended to avoid all such reminders. Gradually, such objects and places tended to lose their hold as the widow accustomed herself to the loss. Evidence of this kind of behaviour among the unemployed also exists.

(3) *Perceptual set.* After reviewing a number of studies of searching behaviour in animals, Parkes observed that when seeking behaviour was evoked at high intensity, finding behaviour tended to occur even in the absence of the object sought. This phenomenon tended to manifest itself in his London study cases where widow's misinterpreted sounds around the house as their husband's presence, or when they momentarily misidentified people in the street. Ten of the twenty-two widows in the study reported that they thought they heard or saw their husbands sometime during the first month, and sixteen reported some sense of presence during the same period. Evidence of this and the following category of seeking behaviour can also be found among the unemployed.

(4) *Calling for the lost person.* When infants are separated from their parents they cry and call out for the lost object. This behaviour is an important part of searching and increases the likelihood of finding the lost parent. A similar tendency could be observed in the searching behaviour of the bereaved. They called out for the dead person or burst into tears.

The unemployed we spoke to reflected some of these components in their own behaviour. They experienced a pining for work in the sense that they frequently thought, sometimes with sadness and sometimes with bitterness, about the things they had lost, about those things which in Chapter 4 we referred to as the detachment-losses associated with unemployment. Some of the aspects of work which appeared to be missed most were those which could not easily be replaced by substituting other 'maintenance' activities through the job hunt or household projects. These included status within the organization, being one of the team and being involved in the 'politics' of the work place, and finally the 'creative mastery' associated with the exercise of certain skills at work. A few also reported directing their attention towards their old place of work, listening to gossip and following press reports or, as one person we spoke to told us, choosing between two alternative bus routes the one which 'went past the old place'. The tendency to seek out the past was not always a pleasurable activity; 'I don't know why I do it. It's a bit like biting on an aching tooth. I know it does not make it any better, but somehow I do it anyway.' Parkes' final two components of search behaviour are reflected in the tendency we observed for people to interpret, at least in the early stages of unemployment, any apparent changes in the fortunes of their old company in the most optimistic light, and in the tendency to make themselves visible so as to increase the likelihood that they would be among the first to be recalled (i.e. found).

One man we interviewed commented on a press report that there had been a call for import controls from leaders in the textile industry in the following manner: 'It won't be long now, once the cheap foreign rubbish is kept out we will all be back at work. They [his old employer] will be getting in touch with me soon.' A woman, also in the textile industry, told us that, 'things will buck up soon', and explained how she and some of her old work mates 'dropped in from time to time' (to their previous place of employment) in order to 'make sure we are not forgotten'.

Searching for something new

Unlike the bereaved, whose loved one is irrevocably lost in this life, the unemployed may be able to re-establish themselves in their lost job. Consequently, search behaviour aimed at finding that which has been lost can be successful. However, this kind of search can also inhibit a different kind of search behaviour, one which is aimed at locating a new job rather than re-establishing the individual in his or her old job. This second kind of search behaviour, the search for something new, was also observed by

Parkes in his study of the bereaved. He suggests that where someone has relied on another person to act in many ways as an extension to himself, then the loss of that person can be expected to have the same effect upon his view of the world and his view of himself as if he had lost a part of himself. In other words, the loss of a loved one on whom he had depended was accompanied by a loss of a part of the self. There is, therefore, a need to rebuild a complete identity and re-establish a purpose in life.

Especially in the early stages of grief, the bereaved tend to be preoccupied with the business of searching for the lost one and little energy is left for other interests. The newly bereaved often show little concern for food, sleep, personal appearance, work, or the family. Establishing a new identity only begins when an awareness of and an interest in the outside world re-emerges. Precisely the same applies to the unemployed.

Pursuing the analogous transition associated with bereavement, it is clear that re-establishing oneself in the outside world involves exploring the implications of the new status of widowhood, seeking out an acceptable place in the social hierarchy, finding out how one is viewed by the rest of the world, and assessing one's ability to define and solve problems. In the early stages of bereavement the first response when faced with a new problem tends to be, 'What would my husband have done about this?' but, as Parkes pointed out, the answer to this question is not always apparent and the use of the remembered husband as the ever-present referee tends to diminish with time. It appears that as the old assumptions about how to relate to the life space are proved ineffective and as a fresh set of assumptions are developed, so the old identity dissolves and is replaced by a new and different one.

Similarly the job hunt can involve search behaviour directed either at the objective of re-establishing the individual in his or her previous position or identifying and establishing the individual in a new position. The success of this latter strategy may be inhibited if the individual uses the job hunt in ways that help him or her to deny that his or her equilibrium has been disturbed (see Chapter 3), and that there is a need to establish a new relationship between self and life space. Search behaviour which involves developing and implementing a new occupational self-concept invariably involves putting many cherished assumptions into the melting pot. Bolles (1978; 1980) argues strongly that some form of personal re-evaluation is an essential prerequisite for the successful job search. Recall expectations, however, can be a powerful force inhibiting such a re-evaluation.

To condemn the harbouring of re-call expectations would be too simple a solution for a complex problem. As we will note later when we consider the work of Sheppard and Belitsky, these expectations are frequently well founded. Similarly, censuring all of those people who seem reluctant to let go of old assumptions about themselves may be unhelpful. Some people may need time to manage this process of letting go. They may modify their thinking about themselves in relation to the world of work gradually. To abandon the security of the past too quickly might overwhelm the ability of some individuals to cope with the uncertainty of the future.

AVOIDANCE BEHAVIOUR AND THE JOB SEARCH

The Second World War produced evidence that people in very stressful situations could be pushed beyond their ability to comprehend and manage their predicament. Swank and Marchand (1946) found that some Allied troops involved in the Normandy landings reacted with dull, listless, and apathetic behaviour. Not the behaviour one would expect from people whose lives were at risk. Numerous studies report that in certain situations the individual can be overwhelmed by massive change and respond by blotting out or denying the reality of the situation.

Many observers have noted that avoidance appears to be a common response to a sudden and major change. It is as though there is a limit to the amount of anxiety a person can tolerate, beyond which he or she tends to withdraw, psychologically, from the anxiety producing situation. There is evidence, however, that such 'avoidance' does not necessarily constitute a basic strategy for dealing with the problem, but may form part of a broader strategy of attack. In other words, various defence mechanisms can form an integral part of an 'approach' strategy when the change involved is of a potentially overwhelming magnitude. Parkes (1972) suggests that because repression and other defence processes play a large part in neurotic illness, and because psychoanalysis was developed as a means of helping the patient abandon his or her defences, a somewhat negative view of defences prevails today. There is a tendency to classify defence as a maladaptive response and to underestimate its potential contribution to healthy adjustment. Defences can be employed to regulate the quantity of disabling information an individual can handle at any one time. In those major life changes where almost every facet of a person's identity needs to be reappraised, the task can be tackled bit by bit, so preserving the individual from sudden and total disorganization. The individual lowers his or her defences and deals with as much of the problem as he or she can handle at any one time. The individual then withdraws behind his or her defences until he or she is able to cope with a little more reality. Avoidance or defensive behaviour is often observed as an inhibitory tendency, which, as Parkes observed, by repression, avoidance, postponement, etc., holds back or limits the perception of disturbing stimuli. This occurs alongside approach or attack behaviour which is described by Parkes as a facilitative or reality testing tendency which enhances perception and thought about disturbing stimuli. Thus, the real problem lies not with the existence of avoidance behaviour or denial *per se*, but with those situations where such behaviour becomes so dominant that the natural process of adjustment is blocked. It is not uncommon in the short term for people to delay the commencement of the job search or to consider only forms of employment almost identical with that lost. In the longer term, however, the continuing experience of unemployment may be associated with a fundamental re-think of the individual's position and with less defensive behaviour.

It can be seen, therefore, that not only does the experience of unemployment differ for individuals in terms of such characteristics as the speed of its onset, the certainty associated with its occurrence and whether or not it is seen as irrevocable, and that these characteristics can influence the nature of the job search, but also that the job hunt which normally follows the loss of work can serve a number of functions such as maintenance, search, and denial.

DIFFERENCES IN JOB SEARCH BEHAVIOUR

Sheppard and Belitsky (1966) undertook an interesting study of the job seeking behaviour of unemployed workers in a local labour market within the United States. They found that of the 309 male, blue-collar workers included in their study a few started looking for work before they were laid off, 41 per cent had commenced their search within twenty-four hours of being laid off and that this figure had risen to 62 per cent by the end of the first week. They also found that 22 per cent never started to look for work. Most of the non-seekers adopted this response because they expected a recall to their previous job. In fact, nearly 70 per cent of this group were eventually recalled. In contrast, of the 141 blue-collar women workers included in the study, 60 per cent did not bother to look for new jobs, but only 45 per cent of this group gave expectancies of future recall to their previous jobs as the reason. Many of the women simply reported that they preferred to stay at home – an interesting reflection on the meaning some women attributed to work in this labour market in 1966.

According to Sheppard and Belitsky, expectations about the probability of call-back can affect job seeking behaviour. They found, for example, that many of the people who eventually were recalled exhibited very similar job search behaviour to those who remained unemployed. Of the still unemployed blue-collar workers in their study 40 per cent had approached five or fewer employers. Of all the workers who were subsequently recalled to their previous jobs 40 per cent likewise approached no more than five companies. In contrast, only 22 per cent of those who found new jobs approached so few companies. Most of those who managed to secure new employment approached more than five potential employers. These figures lend support to the view that recall expectations can significantly affect the nature of job search behaviour.

Exploring further the hypothesis that social-psychological factors can determine, at least in part, the nature of job seeking behaviour, Sheppard and Belitsky found a relationship between achievement motivation and job seeking behaviour. They found that the degree of achievement motivation was related to such behaviour as:

(1) the time the worker waits after being laid-off, before starting his or her job search,
(2) the number of different companies considered during the first month of unemployment,
(3) whether or not he or she approaches out of town employers,
(4) whether he or she restricts enquiries to only those companies who are known to be hiring people,

(5) the range of occupations he or she considers, and
(6) the total number of job seeking techniques used.

They found, further, a clear relationship between achievement motivation and job finding success among workers over the age of twenty-two.

Not only can the job hunt serve different functions but, as the results of Sheppard and Belitsky's study suggest, different people can engage in different patterns of job search behaviour. These different approaches to job seeking can significantly influence the individual's ability to secure alternative employment. There is also a growing body of evidence, some of which is reviewed in Chapter 8, indicating that people can be taught how to develop more effective job search strategies.

Ineffective job seeking can discourage those in search of work, and can eventually contribute to a complete cessation of all search behaviour. As we noted in Chapter 3, while rejections from potential employers in the early phases of the job hunt may not greatly influence expectations about getting a job or the energy devoted to the search for work, repeated rejections may become more difficult to ignore and lead first to a state of dissonance in which the individual begins to accept the possibility of not getting a job whilst at the same time refusing to face up to the prospect of life without work. This eventually develops into a new state of consonance in which the individual becomes resigned to the fact that he or she will remain unemployed. This discouraged worker effect is discussed by Schweitzer and Smith (1974). In spite of some of the limitations of data they appear to find strong support for the hypothesis that the experience of an unsuccessful job search increases the propensity to withdraw from the labour force, both immediately and over the longer term. The resulting hard core of long-term unemployed may not engage in any job search behaviour, or may merely engage in an empty ritual of job search in order to comply with some externally imposed requirement, for example, in order to qualify for certain welfare benefits. A prolonged recession is likely to swell the numbers in this hard core category, a group which is likely to require specialized help if its members are ever to rejoin the ranks of the employed. Chapters 8 and 9 discuss ways in which all those who are unemployed can be helped. The acquisition of better job search techniques may not be sufficient in isolation.

Sheppard and Belitsky suggest that some form of psychological orientation may also be required.

The next chapter explores five ways in which the unemployed can be helped. These involve:

(1) enhancing or maintaining the individual's self-esteem and helping him or her manage anxiety and develop more effective problem solving skills,
(2) improving the fit between the individual and his or her life space,
(3) promoting job seeking skills,
(4) developing new work related skills and
(5) developing positive attitudes towards work and acceptable work habits.

8 Helping the unemployed through measures designed to change the individual

*'The important thing
is to pull yourself up by your own hair
to turn yourself inside out
and to see the world with fresh eyes.'*

PETER WEISS, *Marat/Sade*, 1964

The unemployed are a heterogeneous group comprising the able and disabled, young and old, men and women, black and white, unskilled and highly skilled. It includes those who have only recently lost their jobs and those who have been out of work for many years, those who have lost their jobs for the first time and those who have a history of losing their jobs. It also includes young people who have never been employed since leaving full-time education. These are just a few of the many dimensions along which this heterogeneity can be described. Activities which may help some segments of the unemployed population may be irrelevant to others. This chapter cannot hope to present an exhaustive treatment of all the possible ways forward. Given this caveat, however, a broad-brush attempt will be made to examine some of the ways in which the unemployed can be helped.

Society's response to the unemployed is influenced by its attitudes to those out of work. Typically they are seen as outsiders, as deviants who need help to regain their normal status in society. Most efforts to help the unemployed are directed towards helping them prepare for and regain employment. Rarely are they offered help to accept and adjust to the status of being unemployed.

In theory, if not in practice, helping strategies can be grouped into three categories: strategies to change the individual so as to enhance his or her chances of employment; strategies to change the organization in ways that make it easier for the unemployed to adjust to re-employment; and strategies to change society in ways that will increase demand for labour or in ways that will lead to the unemployed being accepted as full, if different, members of society. This chapter reviews some of the literature associated with the first of these three strategies and the next chapter will examine helping the unemployed by attempting to change the organization or society.

CHANGING THE INDIVIDUAL

The individual is the most frequently selected target for change. The State, private agencies, employing organizations, the Church, other charitable bodies and the family all engage in a range of activities designed to help the individual change in ways that will assist him or her to cope with the predicament of unemployment. Such help includes assisting the individual to manage stress and enhance his or her self-esteem, acquire new identities and goals in order to inject some new purpose into their lives, develop job search skills, acquire new occupational skills and develop positive attitudes towards work and acceptable work habits. These activities receive most attention in this chapter because they reflect the strategies most frequently adopted to help the individual cope with unemployment.

SELF-ESTEEM, THE MANAGEMENT OF STRESS AND PROBLEM SOLVING

The ability to manage personal change is influenced by the individual's affective functioning, by his or her level of self-esteem and his or her ability to cope effectively with negative feelings. Many activities designed to help the unemployed have included attempts to improve the individual's image of him- or herself. Loss of work may present a serious threat to the individual's self-esteem and promote attitudes towards self that make a return to normal working life difficult. Hartmann (1972) notes that a central assumption underlying the work of the industrial rehabilitation units in the UK is that rehabilitation positively influences attitudes towards self. Testing this assump-

tion he constructed two scales, one to measure keenness for work
and the other to assess a composite of attitudes which he labelled
'inadequacy', and which included feelings of inferiority, insecurity, loss of self-respect, and self-esteem. He found that an
eight-week course at an industrial rehabilitation unit led to a
reduction in feelings of inadequacy, thus supporting the assumption that rehabilitation may help to restore a person's self-
confidence, improve the self-image, reduce anxiety and feelings
of insecurity, etc. It was interesting to note, however, that
Hartmann's study did not reveal any changes in the client's
keenness for work, a theme which has already been discussed in
Chapter 4 and one which will be taken up later in this chapter.

Tiffany, Cowan, and Tiffany (1970) adopt a phenomenological
stance and argue that the self-concept is a potent determiner of
behaviour in so far as it influences the way people view the world.
Schlien (1963), they feel, puts the point well when he states that
the interpretation of self leads to a reactive interpretation of the
external object.

> 'For instance, if one feels strong, a boulder is a weapon to push
> into the treads of an armoured tank, if weak, the same boulder
> is a refuge to hide behind. If one feels sick and helpless, the
> nurse is a creature of mercy, appealed to for comfort. The same
> nurse may be seen as a temptress, to be sexually pursued, if the
> patient sees himself as well and sturdy. All experience is
> evaluated as friendly or dangerous, interesting or boring,
> possible, etc. depending not upon the nature of the experience
> so much as upon the *self concept of the experiencer*.
>   (Cited in Tiffany, Cowan and Tiffany 1970:90)

Tiffany, Cowan, and Tiffany found that when they administered
the Tennessee self-concept scale to thirty-one subjects with
interrupted work histories which included long periods of unemployment, and also to a socio-economically comparable group
who had been in steady employment for twelve months, there
were marked differences in the profiles of the two groups. The
profile of the unemployed group reflected their low level of self-
esteem compared to the employed group. They saw themselves as
undesirable, doubted their worth, often felt anxious, depressed,
and unhappy, and had little faith or confidence in themselves. A
state of affairs reflected in our discussion in Chapter 6.

Fineman (1979) presents a phenomenological model of stress

which postulates that the meaning the individual places on particular potential stress stimuli and the affective reactions to them, depend on the individual view of self in relation to the demands which are characteristically made on him or her. Studying a group of unemployed managers he found that those who were highly stressed were less successful in locating employment than those who experienced only low levels of stress. His research indicated that high stress elicited less effective coping responses, such as avoidance and inactivity, whereas lower levels of stress tended to elicit more effective coping responses such as confrontation. Fineman hypothesized that problems perceived as threatening to the self are potential stressors, that very low levels of self-esteem increase the individual's susceptibility for experiencing environmental demands as threatening and that low levels of self-esteem are associated with feelings of incompetence to deal with the environment. He also postulated a possible downward spiral in which the experience of stress could further erode feelings of competence and self-esteem. This model leads one to conclude that there is some substance behind the assumption, underlying the many programmes to help the unemployed, that improving self-esteem is an important intermediate goal. Fineman's model identifies a clear relationship between the individual's level of self-esteem and the ability to master problems, particularly problems associated with unemployment. The importance of self-esteem has been underlined by Hodgson and Brenner (1968), Allerhand *et al.* (1969) and Teahan (1969) all of whom found a relationship between self-esteem and the work behaviour of the newly hired long-term unemployed.

THE ACQUISITION OF NEW IDENTITIES, PURPOSES AND GOALS

Loss of work involves a major change in the way an individual relates to the world. As noted in Chapter 4, it deprives a person of a place of work, the company of workmates, an area of activity and interest, a source of income, a sense of purpose, and a source of identity and self-esteem. It produces a multitude of changes in the assumptions the individual makes about him- or herself and the way of relating with the environment. Assumptions about how each day is to be spent, about sources of income, and even about the capacity to work effectively and earn a living will be challenged. In short, the assumptions the individual makes about his or her identity as a person will be under pressure. Adjustment to loss of work involves attempts to re-establish a good fit between the individual and his or her environment. Instead of constantly looking over their shoulders and clinging to past identities, individuals have to take stock of themselves in relation to their new predicament and search for a fresh and more appropriate fit. This involves coming to terms with the reality that things have changed. Where a change is experienced as a loss the process of letting go of old assumptions and identities can be a difficult and sometimes painful one.

Life planning and personal re-evaluation workshops have been used as a vehicle for helping the individual take stock and manage personal change. A basic assumption underlying this approach is that the individual's concept of self not only organizes the way self is seen in relation to the world, but also motivates the individual into taking action.

Super (1953) views the process of vocational development as one in which the individual develops and then implements a concept of himself or herself. According to Super, this is a compromise process in which the self-concept is a product of the interaction of inherited aptitudes, neural and endocrine make-up, opportunity to play various roles, and evaluations of the extent to which the results of role playing meet with approval of supervisors and colleagues. This process begins very early in life. As the child develops and as its range of experience widens it begins to find that it is both like and unlike other people and it begins to realize that it is a distinct person in its own right. Through experience and self-examination it acquires and clarifies a mental picture of itself – the self-concept. When it tries out its self-concept in various situations it finds that while some facets are rewarded and win approval, others are punished and do not. It therefore tends to retain and reinforce those aspects of the self-concept which are rewarded and bring gratification, and to reject the others. Throughout life individuals will seek outlets which will give them the opportunity to play the kind of role which is in harmony both with the way in which they see themselves and the way they would like to be seen. They are drawn towards those activities which offer the promise of projecting the image they would like others to have of them. For many people being a member of the work force is an important part of that image and the individual is motivated to maintain it. When deprived of the opportunity to work the individual's concept of self is sabotaged and he or she is in danger of losing his or her sense of purpose.

Life planning and personal re-evaluation help people to re-examine themselves and use the resultant revised concepts of self to develop new life and career goals. The major contributor to the life planning approach has been Herbert A. Shepard, but more recently Hopson (1976) has developed a series of workshops which provide a structured opportunity for individuals, working alone and in mutual support groups, to answer the following questions for themselves:

(1) Who am I and where am I now?
(2) How did I get here?
(3) How satisfied am I with who I am and where I am?
(4) How would I like to change my life and myself?
(5) How rational are these desires?
(6) How do I accomplish these changes?

Allen (1975) has identified the aims of life planning and personal re-evaluation in terms of creating:

(1) changes in internal cognitive functioning, e.g. understanding one's behaviour and the reasons for it better,
(2) changes in internal affective functioning, e.g. coping with negative feelings more effectively, feeling more positive about oneself, and
(3) changes in externally observable behaviour, e.g. creating or taking opportunities.

These aims do not necessarily imply that life planning and personal re-evaluation will always help the individual develop new and more appropriate occupational self-concepts that will lead to the generation of more appropriate career strategies. While this may be the outcome for many people the individual may also begin to think more about self in non-career terms and may develop life goals that do not involve a traditional work career. In other words it is an approach that can, if used with care, help the individual begin to adjust to the prospect of long-term unemployment. In a different context, Kelly (1980) notes that it offers a way to encourage people to think positively about and plan for their retirement. While the authors are unaware of any empirical studies which have evaluated the effectiveness of life planning, they have encountered a wealth of anecdotal evidence which indicates that many people have found it useful.

Counselling on a one-to-one basis is another way of achieving these related goals. It can be used in three ways to help the individual cope with change. Counselling can serve an *adjustive* function and be used to help people develop a more appropriate balance between their self-concept and their career. Tyler (1961), discussing the problems of adjusting aspirations downwards, argued the need to develop counselling situations that facilitated attitude change, and suggested that by working in situations rich in acceptance and understanding, so that defensiveness is minimized and the person is able to grasp and accept his or her own limitations, realism and clear thinking may gradually win over inflated expectations. In practice the client's hostility towards the helper, his or her distrust of officials in general, together with the crisis element in the situation may not be very conducive to the development of Tyler's acceptant climate. For some clients, therefore, an alternative approach to adjustive counselling may be required. One such approach is confrontation where the counsellor takes nothing for granted, constantly probes and challenges the assumptions made by the client, presents counter arguments and facts, but attempts to do so in a way that does not make the client too defensive and resistant to change. Counselling can also serve a *motivational* function to arouse and stimulate new ways of thinking about careers. Whether it be the ambitious or the steady plodders who find themselves unemployed, both might be encouraged to explore possible alternatives, the kinds of boundaries these alternatives would present and the action necessary to successfully cross them. Finally, counselling can serve an *evaluative* function and help people assess for themselves their needs and explore how these might best be satisfied. In this way the counsellor can help the client evaluate different opportunities and decide which, if any, to pursue.

ACQUISITION OF JOB SEARCH SKILLS

The previous chapter discussed job search behaviour. Some people are much more successful at finding jobs than others and this success does not always reflect their job skills. Some very able workers may fail to secure employment simply because they do not use effective job search strategies, or because they fail to communicate an attractive image to potential employers. People can be helped to enhance their attractiveness by preparing résumés, application forms, and letters of application in ways that present themselves in the most favourable light, by researching the requirements of potential employers, and by learning to present and manage themselves at interview. However, all this effort will be wasted unless they can locate organizations that are looking for labour. They must, therefore, also learn to search out job opportunities.

These skills can be learned. They can be learned on courses and they can also be learned through self-help exercises and books. Books like Bolles' *What Colour is Your Parachute?* have begun to appear, together with television series and job search packs. In the UK Westward Television and the National Extension College Trust have co-operated to produce *Just the Job* and associated 'job hunter kits' and the Schools Council has produced a series of ten job search booklets for use by counsellors, teachers, youth workers, careers officers, and social workers who have the opportunity of gathering groups of school leavers or unemployed young people together. The aim is to help young people find jobs for themselves. To do this, group sessions are arranged in order to unite young people who may have become isolated and dispirited in their search for work in order to enable them to work together, share resources, and assist each other with the problems of unemployment. The schools council booklets provide a stimulus for group discussions, but also provide something that young people can take away and use to help them do something about their own situation.

Formal courses designed to improve job search skills have been found to be successful with a wide range of trainees. Shapiro (1978) reports a study on a programme that was open to any Cambridge (Mass.) resident who had been unemployed for at least six months, had vocational abilities exceeding the semi-skilled level and who had no obvious employment impediments. She found that 69 per cent of the participants in this four-week programme found work compared with 33 per cent of the control group, a difference that was significant at the 0.001 level. She attributed this success to the higher number of interviews that were secured by participants in the programme and the effect this had on their self-esteem.

Powell (1973) reports on a job strategy seminar for people at the upper end of the labour market, for unemployed engineers and scientists. He found that lack of practice and discouragement were two problems that seemed to prevent them from finding jobs. Twenty-two subjects participated in ten group meetings which combined didactic and self-analytic features. When compared to a matched control group the experimental group showed significant differences in several areas. Eleven members of the experimental group were successful in locating jobs within ninety days of the end of the seminars, compared with six members of the control group. The experimental group were more active in the number of visits they made to Harvard's job bank and to placement agencies, and tended to have more interviews in the follow up period. Like Shapiro, Powell also identified a link between self-image and job seeking behaviour and found that the experimental group made more positive and fewer negative statements about themselves than did members of the control group.

Bowser, Sherman, and Whisler (1974) looked at a very different population, the unattached, chronically unemployed males who tend to congregate in any central city community. The early phases of the programme they investigated focused on helping participants develop broad employment goals and specific job objectives. Emphasis was then switched to developing abilities to locate and apply for existing job openings. An underlying aim throughout the programme was to help the chronically unemployed acquire the self-assurance necessary to utilize these skills.

Men who were referred to the employment unit of the Unattached Men's Center of the Los Angeles Department of Public Social Services were interviewed and tested and asked to return the following Monday. Of those who returned 12–15 were randomly selected each week for training. Over the duration of the programme 179 men embarked on the training (project starters) and 462 were tested and interviewed but received no training (non-participants). While both groups were broadly similar there were some differences which could be accounted for by the element of self-selection which determined who turned up the following Monday. For example, both groups (project starters and non-participants) evidenced feelings of anger and hostility towards authorities or society in general, combined with feelings of being exploited and persecuted by others, and feelings of alienation and aloneness. However, one area of difference reported by Bowser, Sherman, and Whisler was that the starters showed less indication of alienation, helplessness, and depression than the non-participants, and in general seemed to be psychologically healthier.

During the follow-up period 7 per cent of the non-participant group secured employment compared with 42 per cent of the project starters. However, if the 60 project starters who dropped out before the completion of the project are eliminated then 83 per cent of the trainees secured employment. Of these, 51 per cent secured employment within 14 days of completing the programme and over 80 per cent accepted positions equal to or better than their previous job. Criterion measures before and after training also indicate that the trainees experienced significant positive changes in their self-image.

These findings support the view that a relationship exists between self-esteem and the ability to master problems. They also indicate that attempts to help the unemployed secure work by enhancing their job search skills can be successful for a wide range of subjects. However, there is also evidence which relates back to the discussion in Chapters 4 and 7 that some of the long-term unemployed are not especially motivated to seek or accept help in this respect.

NEW JOB SKILLS

Most countries in the western world have elaborate training provisions designed to equip the unemployed with new job skills. Such training can be offered before the individual is released onto the labour market, while he or she is unemployed and, in some cases, after he or she has commenced work for a new employer. It can also embrace a wide range of trainees from the out-of-work manager and professional worker to the unskilled and even the hard core unemployed.

Warr and Lovatt (1977) report on a programme of pre-redundancy training which was associated with the closure of the British Steel plant at Irlam. Over 2000 people, mostly men, were laid-off. Following British Steel's policy, considerable notice of the closure had been given and every employee was provided with the opportunity of having at least two personnel counselling interviews during the year preceding closure. These interviews focused on the financial payments he would receive and on the possible paths he might follow after redundancy. One of the issues frequently discussed was the value to the individual of different types of training. Two kinds were available: courses which normally lasted several months at one of the government run skill centres, geared to providing important basic skills; and courses developed by the British Steel Corporation designed to increase the employees' ability to obtain jobs after redundancy. Some of these were arranged in the works and others were provided by outside agencies. Most of the ninety-nine employees who applied for courses at government run skill centres were unable to commence their training before the plant closure; however, all the Corporation's courses were planned to take place before the date of closure. Three hundred and sixty-five employees attended these pre-closure courses, and six different courses were available in machining, arc welding, motor vehicle repair, heavy goods vehicle driving and construction industry training.

An interview follow up six months after closure revealed that significantly more pre-closure trainees were in employment. It was also found that some 12 per cent of trainees were in jobs which they could not have undertaken without pre-closure training and some 30 per cent indicated that they were using their training in some way. The researchers also discovered some other benefits in terms of increased confidence and wider experience which could not be quantified, but which again pointed to the importance of promoting or maintaining the self-esteem of those who are to lose their jobs.

Warr and Lovatt (1977) argue that in cases of irreversible redundancy, where there is a greater need for personal readjustment, retraining is particularly worth considering. They point out, however, that extensive retraining is not a realistic alternative for more than a small number of people and, where it is offered, it needs to be linked to a system of individual counselling. In this way training can be devised to meet the needs of the individual within the context of the local market. They also speculate about the possible scope of a multi-tier training arrangement for people prior to redundancy. Each might have different objectives, thus high level courses could be specifically oriented to the transmission of new skills, whereas lower tier courses could embrace procedures that would familiarize people with different industries and alert them to their own retraining potential.

In the UK the government now offers a wide range of training for those out of work at all levels. Whereas in the past the focus of training has tended to be on rehabilitating the disabled through the industrial rehabilitation centres and on manual skills through skill centres, today the government offers a broad spectrum of training at colleges and employers' establishments. The schemes embrace a wide range of courses ranging from those for redundant executives and technicians to those for the skilled and unskilled manual and clerical workers. Consideration is also being given to an expansion of 'employment rehabilitation' to embrace, in addition to the disabled, the able bodied with other special handicaps.

The term 'hard core unemployed' has been used in the USA and in Canada to describe those individuals who have a history of being unable to obtain and/or retain regular employment. It is sometimes used more specifically to describe the economically disadvantaged who can be classified as being in one of the following categories: school drop out, minority member, under twenty-two years of age, over forty-five years of age, or handicapped. Training for the hard core has focused on job skills and on work attitudes.

Researchers have used different criterion variables to evaluate the success of job skills training for the hard core unemployed. Kirchner and Lucas (1972) focused attention on the proportion of trainees who completed training, and were transferred from the training centre to a regular job, implying that for the hard core that in itself was a measure of success. They studied 128 male trainees in the 3M Company's Factory Training Center. Low income was the only criterion for acceptance, ensuring a highly heterogeneous sample. The overall success rate was 25 per cent, but it was found that older workers were more likely to succeed than younger workers – an outcome which they largely attributed to motivation.

Salipante and Goodman (1976) evaluated the success of training in terms of the numbers of trainees who were retained in regular employment. This appears to be a valuable criterion variable in the light of Goodale's (1973) observation that of the first 400,000 employees hired as part of the jobs programme (Job Opportunities in the Business Sector) in the USA, 47 per cent quit their jobs within the first six months of employment. Salipante and Goodman's data were drawn from 180 training programmes organized by 114 firms. This clearly differentiated their study from most others, which examined effects of a particular programme in a single company. Their main finding was that there was no simple relationship between training and retention. Their results indicated that it was the content of training, rather than whether training was offered, that was the critical variable.

Job skills training was positively related to retention whereas some kinds of aptitudinal training was negatively related to retention. (However, it was also found that with those programmes in which the level of job skills training accounted for more than 80 per cent of the overall training content the retention rate was lower.) Salipante and Goodman explained this positive relationship between job-skill training and retention in terms of expectancy theory. They hypothesized that job-skills training provides the individual with a direct set of experiences that enhance his or her belief (expectancy) that he or she can perform the job effectively. Furthermore, by practising the job he or she hopes to do, the individual's distrust of the company's intentions will be reduced and his or her belief (instrumentality) about the availability of a job will be strengthened.

WORK ATTITUDES AND WORK BEHAVIOUR

Efforts to help the unemployed develop 'normal' work values and acquire appropriate work habits tend to be focused on two main groups, the long-term unemployed and the unemployed school leaver.

The development of positive attitudes towards work is one of the fundamental objectives that underlies many of the provisions for unemployed school leavers. Most schemes take the form of either special training courses or the creation of temporary employment opportunities. Many of the courses for unemployed school leavers are similar to those provided for the hard core unemployed that will be discussed below. They focus on the development of an understanding of the culture of the work environment, the development of good work habits and positive work values. They also embrace some of the objectives already discussed, such as the acquisition of job search skills and the development of particular occupational skills. Some courses for young people also place emphasis on exposing participants to a range of job opportunities, and providing realistic occupational information in order to facilitate the development of new or revised career objectives and to stimulate or maintain purposeful work-oriented behaviour. Most of these 'course' objectives are also pursued through job creation programmes and work experience schemes.

The precise forms these measures take differ from country to country but in the UK, at the time of writing, they include the Youth Opportunities Programme (YOP) which is directed at those aged sixteen to eighteen who have been unemployed for at least six weeks. Because the programme is aimed at the needs of young people from a wide range of backgrounds, and with different abilities and interests, it embraces various measures designed to reflect the differing needs and circumstances of participants. They include three types of work preparation programme and four types of work experience scheme. In 1978/79 about 80 per cent of the approved places on YOP were provided through work experience schemes and of these 'Work Experience on Employers' Premises' was the most important. Follow up surveys of this kind of work experience scheme were carried out in 1977 and 1978 (Manpower Services Commission 1979). The 1977 survey interviewed people five months after leaving the programme and the 1978 survey interviewed people after seven months. In 1977 65 per cent of the participants, and in 1978 72 per cent of the participants, went straight into employment. At the time of the survey 75 per cent were employed in 1977 and 80 per cent were employed in 1978. Approximately half of those in employment at the time of the survey were still working with the employer who had sponsored them.

Many people who leave full-time education and find themselves unemployed are over the age of eighteen. In the UK these young adults may be eligible for help under the Special Temporary Employment Programme (STEP), which provides temporary jobs on projects of benefit to the community. This programme is exclusively for adults, and while people aged twenty-five and over have to be unemployed for twelve months before they qualify, young adults between the ages of nineteen and twenty-four are eligible when they have been unemployed for six months.

Community industry is another scheme specially aimed at unemployed young people who for various reasons find it difficult to obtain or keep jobs. This scheme places special emphasis on those young people who are personally or socially disadvantaged, and is designed to provide a rehabilitative element aimed at improving skills, knowledge, and behaviour in order to prepare participants for ordinary work.

While it may be difficult to assess the real success of some of these measures, especially since they simultaneously pursue a number of different aims, there can be little doubt that they do foster the idea that employment is a more desirable state than unemployment. They socialize young people into accepting the work ethic. Although it is conceivable that a continuing rise in unemployment may lead to a situation in which society has to help young people build their futures without paid employment, within the prevailing culture and with 1980 levels of unemployment it is not surprising that governments give priority to measures which promote the work ethic among the young unemployed.

DIFFICULTIES ASSOCIATED WITH ATTEMPTS TO CHANGE WORK VALUES

Attempts to modify the work attitudes and work habits of the adult hard core unemployed through the use of specially designed courses have met with mixed results. Salipante and Goodman (1976), as already mentioned, discovered a negative relationship between attitudinal training, as measured by the incidence of role playing, and retention, and Allerhand *et al.* (1969) and Frank (1969) both failed to establish any clear relationship between training and changes in certain attitudinal and motivational dimensions.

Goodale (1973) considered the difficulties associated with attempting to change work values through orientation courses. He advanced the view that it was unlikely that a relatively short course could change work values that had been formed by many years of experience. He also pointed out that many of the jobs for which the disadvantaged were prepared were routine and un-stimulating and not likely to reinforce a set of work values that projected work as intrinsically rewarding. He also indicated that the hard core might become disillusioned with their jobs when expectations formed in training were not fulfilled. Supporting this speculation is the finding of Quinn, Fine, and Levitin (1970) that training could raise expectations beyond the realities of the work situation. Quinn, Fine and Levitin found that trained individuals frequently preferred more autonomy than they experienced on entry level jobs, and they perceived the quality of supervision as lower than those who had not received orientation training.

Friedlander and Greenberg (1971) also reported results which support the case that attempts to change work habits and values through orientation training will be unsuccessful. Nine attitude scales measuring motivation to work, motivation to avoid work, motivation to avoid unemployment, perception of previous job, importance of job characteristics, prized self-image, powerlessness, cynicism, and vigour were administered to trainees who participated in a two-week orientation programme. Each participant was assigned to a counsellor cum trainer who worked with him both individually and in groups. The content of the programmes included human relations, job orientation, money management and budgeting, physical fitness, and transportation (the use of public transport systems to reach job sites). No significant changes in attitude were recorded between either the first or last day of the orientation programme or between the last day of the orientation programme and, after employment experiences, six months later. Friedlander and Greenberg concluded that neither the orientation programme nor the subsequent job experience fostered a more adaptive attitude towards work.

THE RELATIVE SUCCESS OF DIFFERENT APPROACHES TO WORK ORIENTATION TRAINING

Other studies using retention as the criterion have reported some success. Rosen and Turner (1971) compared the relative effectiveness of two approaches to work orientation training. Effectiveness was judged in terms of turnover and absenteeism. Comparisons were made between the hard core employees in two treatment conditions, university-sponsored quasi-therapeutic orientation and company-sponsored orientation, and between hard core hires and normal hires. Overall the hard core hires were not differentiated from normal hires in terms of turnover but were characterized by significantly higher absenteeism; however the company-oriented programme for the hard core unemployed was superior to the quasi-therapeutic programme in developing stable employees. In fact, Rosen and Turner concluded that given an appropriate programme of orientation training the hard core can turn out to be as stable as people hired *via* normal hiring channels, who satisfy established selection criteria.

The company-oriented programme contained subject matter that was job oriented and crucial to acceptable work behaviour. Possible benefits that could be derived from working with the company were outlined and important rules, and the penalties for their infraction, were repeatedly emphasized. The rationale behind these rules was also discussed. Another important feature of the company-oriented programme was the direct access the training supervisor had to the organization, and the fact that he represented the company to the trainees. He knew the rules and could assess them realistically. He could even interpret them from the perspective of the supervisors who would be implementing them. Thus, given a problem employee, he could not only communicate to that person the consequences of certain behaviour, but could and did intercede with his or her supervisor on his or her behalf. This important liaison function was not incorporated within the quasi-therapeutic programme.

On the university-sponsored programme the trainees established their own content, much of which was not directly relevant to their jobs or work in general. In spite of the efforts of the trainer, work problems were brushed aside in favour of broader issues related to life in general. The trainer was not familiar with company practices and policies and was not in a position to intercede for the trainee either to clarify rule enforcement standards or to request a temporary, less rigorous rule enforcement.

One apparent conclusion from this study seems to be that to be effective, orientation training needs to be related to specific jobs, an argument in favour of post-commencement job orientation training. There are, however, examples of orientation training that have been successful and that have been organized before the trainees have been offered employment. Shandy and Kuc (1977) report a study in Winnipeg of a six-week social skills orientation course for the hard core unemployed. In line with the philosophy of other courses such as the Minneapolis Rehabilitation Centre (Cull and Hardy 1973) jobs were not found for trainees, but help in developing the self-confidence, employment goals, and contacts with potential employers essential for securing employment were an integral part of the course. The first week was largely concerned with orienting participants to the programme, and included exercises aimed at developing communication skills, understanding the value of work, and discovering personal strengths and problem solving abilities. The second week focused on working with others and, towards the end of the week, examined money management and budgeting. The focus changed in the third and fourth weeks and was strongly geared to specific employment related issues such as practising interviews, identifying employment sources, practising job applications, discussing expectations of employers, and developing creative job search techniques. In fact dealing with the kind of issues characteristic of programmes designed to develop job search strategies which have been discussed above. An interesting feature of the course was the fifth 'work week', during which participants offered their services to employers while the social skills orientation course continued to pay the minimum wage that participants received throughout the course. Those who had not secured permanent employment returned for a sixth week of review and further job searching. Personal counselling was available throughout the programme. Of the 213 participants, 169 completed and 44 terminated before the end of the programme. A follow-up study involving 105 of the trainees revealed that 67 per cent of those who completed were employed. The success rate was maintained over the fifteen months of the follow up study. Of those who quit the programme only 21 per cent were employed over this period. These results demonstrate a very strong association between completing the programme and full-time employment ($P = 0.0001$). It is worth noting, however, that although this training was pre-commencement every effort was made to relate the programme to immediate employment opportunities, and to motivate trainees to take responsibility for their own behaviour.

Hutson and Smith (1969) provide an earlier example of a programme organized away from the employing organization that was relatively successful as measured by retention over the short term. (Six weeks after completing the programme 11 of the 12 graduates were still employed.) Four features of this programme are of interest. Firstly, the programme staff were not professional educators. The programme co-ordinator was a blue-collar worker and other resource people were former hard core unemployed, line managers and representatives of unions, personnel, and other specialized functions. The aim of involving these people was to promote an environment that was conducive to obtaining group involvement. Secondly, the content of the programme was structured and very specifically oriented to work related issues. Thirdly applicants were each allocated a sponsor cum counsellor who accompanied the trainee to job interviews, helped work out transportation problems and liaised with the employer after the trainee started work. Finally, before the training commenced all applicants were helped to find jobs which were offered to them on condition that they successfully completed the training. Hutson and Smith argued that to offer training without the promise of employment was to invite a further deterioration in the work attitudes of the unemployed.

Another issue raised by the Rosen and Turner study was the choice of training method. Rosen and Turner found that the university-sponsored, quasi-therapeutic treatment was ineffective, and in a later study Salipante and Goodman found that attitude training which focused on role play was negatively related to retention.

Role play

O'Leary (1972) on the basis of Cooley's (1922) notion of reflexive identification, assumed that role playing would be a promising means of achieving the kind of shift in self-concept and concomitant changes in attitudes towards work that would ease the cultural transition back into the world of work for the hard core unemployed. She thought that role play would provide the new hire with an opportunity to learn what to expect in interactions with supervisors, together with an opportunity to observe and experience problems from the supervisors' point of view, thereby gaining insight into the necessity for rule enforcement. She found, however, that while subjects in her experimental condition did incidence greater positive changes in attitudes towards self there was no evidence of a positive shift in attitudes towards work. An important implication seems to be that role play training aimed at re-socialization that does not take into account the nature of the job as well as the target population may be ineffective, or as Salipante and Goodman (1976) found, even detrimental. The subjects in O'Leary's study were employed in a structured, tedious work situation which offered few opportunities for communicating with others. Reflexive role playing that demonstrates or verifies to the trainee that his or her work is indeed tedious or unrewarding may raise questions about whether or not to continue performing such work. If the training has raised the trainees' level of self-esteem the trainee may react by leaving and seeking alternative work more compatible with his or her new expectations. As Quinn, Fine, and Levitin (1970) discovered, care has to be taken not to raise expectations beyond the realities of the work situation.

Social conditioning

This is one approach to promoting successful adjustment to work that seems to have received relatively little attention but which promises to have great potential. Sandler and Turner (1973) report an interesting attempt to apply Ayllon and Azrin's (1968) token economy approach to rehabilitation to the vocational rehabilitation of the long-term unemployed. Specific training programmes were devised for each client or trainee which specified long-term and intermediate objectives that would promote changes in the desired direction. Successful attainment of these objectives earned the trainee tokens which could be redeemed later for cash. Immediate positive reinforcement for suitable behaviour was a cornerstone of this approach. Sandler and Turner's evaluation focused on the subsequent employment record of trainees (retention) and behaviour changes which occurred during training.

Within the first year of operation 179 trainees were placed in employment. Twenty-six months after the start of the programme these trainees were invited to participate in a follow up study. Of the 127 trainees who participated 69 per cent indicated that they were still in employment.

Sandler and Turner illustrated the kinds of behaviour change that occurred and the way the programme operated with the aid of a number of case studies. One case involved a thirty-three-year-old divorcee with three dependent children. As a result of poliomyelitis she wore a brace and used crutches. When she entered the programme certain problem conditions were identified and defined including poor personal appearance and excessive demands for attention and sympathy from all staff members and other clients. A specific programme involving her counsellor, social worker, and re-education and community aids was formulated and, in addition, all staff members were instructed to praise the client when she dressed appropriately and to ignore all her demands for attention by directing her to designated individuals. After two months sufficient progress was made for her to secure employment and a follow-up six months later revealed she was maintaining satisfactory work performance.

A very different kind of case involved an eighteen-year-old student who had been suspended from school after experiencing problems with a number of teachers and finally threatening to kill one of them. An initial assessment revealed a high incidence of negative behaviour when he was assigned tasks, few social skills, and a strong resistance to participating in the re-education programme. The first objective of his rehabilitation programme was simply to increase the length of time he spent in the classroom. He was told that he would earn tokens simply by coming to class even if he did not join in any of the classroom activities. The length of time required in the classroom for receiving tokens was gradually increased from several minutes to two hours. A second objective was to reduce the frequency with which he engaged in inappropriate verbal behaviour. His teachers were instructed to ignore any negative comments and inappropriate demands for attention, but to respond to him when his actions indicated a serious interest in the teacher-assigned task. This combination of tokens and praise resulted in a substantial improvement in behaviour. The final objective was to motivate him to participate in classroom activities. By the tenth session this objective was largely achieved and he was participating for approximately 90 per cent of each two-hour period. On completion of his programme the client was transferred to an adult day high school where he completed his high school education without difficulty.

A third case illustrates how this approach can be applied even where the basic problems appear to be family centred. The principal client was a thirty-two-year-old divorcee with three daughters who declared that she was unable to seek or maintain employment because of high blood pressure which was a result of serious difficulties at home. A number of home-based problems were confirmed by a social worker. Her seventeen-year-old daughter was already the mother of one child and was pregnant with another. Her sixteen-year-old daughter also had a child and, in spite of a good school record, had dropped out of high school. The youngest daughter was experiencing behaviour problems at school and had already been expelled several times. In addition to serious financial difficulties the social worker reported that the children made little effort to assist the mother in the household tasks and displayed only a minimum of interest in caring for their children. A family-centred programme was designed to facilitate the development of a co-operative household within which each member would assume responsibility for certain tasks. The older daughter was given responsibility for caring for the babies and the two younger daughters were assigned responsibility for about 75 per cent of the household chores. Tokens were paid on the completion of the required tasks. The mother's responsibility was to engage in a re-education programme and, at the same time, supervise the efforts of her daughters. Bonuses were given when everybody worked in a co-operative manner. The principal client completed her re-education programme and, against the background of a family programme that was by then functioning without difficulty, secured employment that she retained throughout the period of the follow-up study.

The social conditioning approach appeared to result in important changes within a relatively short period of time (a typical client was involved in the programme for about six weeks), and success was achieved with a variety of problems. Working towards explicit job-oriented goals, programmes could be written which took into account the special needs of each client. These programmes frequently involved home-based and educational intermediate goals as a pathway to successful vocational rehabilitation. An important feature of this particular approach was that it promoted consistency of effort between all personnel dealing with a client. Another feature, which seemed to be shared in some way by all successful training activities, was the location of responsibility for affecting change. This was placed squarely on the trainee's shoulders. The trainee proceeded at his or her own pace and retained control over how much change was accomplished. This control was facilitated by the provision of immediate feedback regarding progress.

Feedback

The provision of feedback was central to Hartlage and Johnson's (1971) attempt to develop appropriate work behaviour among the hard core unemployed. Testing the hypothesis that the provision of video taped self-confrontation would improve production and time spent working, they treated twenty subjects with video feedback and twenty with conventional concept-oriented counselling. The subjects receiving the video treatment had random portions of their work behaviour filmed each day and participated in a fifteen-minute video feedback session of each day's behaviour on the subsequent work day. Occasional voice comments calling attention to desirable or undesirable behaviours were superimposed on the video tapes. The remaining twenty subjects received fifteen to twenty minutes traditional counselling each day, with the content of the sessions oriented towards a recapitulation of the preceding day's work behaviour. After only fifteen days exposure to video tape play-back the experimental group demonstrated a significant improvement over base line measures in both productivity and time spent working, whereas controls failed to demonstrate significant improvements on either variable.

The liaison-counselling role

In addition to the possible implications of the choice of training method, Rosen and Turner also drew attention to the liaison-counselling role of the training supervisor. The importance of counselling was also confirmed by Salipante and Goodman, who found that counselling appeared to strengthen beliefs about the desirability of coming to work and counteract some of the negative effects associated with training. For example, they found that while retention was negatively related to length of training, this effect was counteracted by the presence of extensive counselling.

In organizational terms the counsellors in both studies occupied rather special roles. They could be observed spanning organizational boundaries: working outside the organization, across departmental boundaries, and at different levels in the hierarchy in an attempt to offer personal support to the trainees, influence perceptions that the company was interested in them, and that they had the ability to be good employees. They also worked to reduce the tension and conflict between trainees and supervisors, and generally to affect the valence of working for trainees. To be effective, this role required the kind of organizational access normally denied to the traditional vocational guidance counsellor.

While there is no uniformity of research design or of results in the research we have examined, a number of conclusions about effective work orientation training programmes do appear to be warranted. They are

(1) *job orientation* – successful programmes seem to be associated with the preparation for a specific job rather than work in general and are seen by trainees to lead to guaranteed employment;

(2) *training methods* – some methods, such as role play and self-directed discussion groups, appear to be less successful than those which involve work experience, feedback on progress towards work related goals and immediate and positive reinforcement;

(3) *liaison and support* – a number of studies report that counselling and liaison between the training and work setting is frequently associated with success;

(4) *identity and experience of training staff* – some studies indicate that professional educators, especially those based in universities and colleges, appear to be less effective than resource persons who have, or are seen to have, a more intimate knowledge and understanding of the immediate work environment;

(5) *course content* – more success appears to be reported when attention is focused on work attitudes and work behaviour rather than upon more general issues such as those associated with being disadvantaged and unemployed.

Vocational rehabilitation which focuses on the development of positive attitudes towards work and on the development of effective work behaviour can, under certain circumstances, be successful and, it would seem, can be achieved in a relatively short period of time. Furthermore, there is evidence (Salipante and Goodman) that attempts to help the long-term unemployed develop job skills which ignore trainee's work attitudes are likely to be less successful than programmes that embrace both dimensions.

CONCLUSION

This chapter has examined a number of the ways in which the individual can be changed in an attempt to ameliorate the effects of unemployment. The underlying assumption appears to be that every effort should be made to enhance the individual's chance of regaining employment. Relatively little emphasis has been given, in the literature, to helping the individual come to terms with the transition from work to unemployment. The implicit assumption appears to be that unemployment for a particular individual will only be a temporary state.

This emphasis on helping the individual change in order to improve his or her chances of securing re-employment may be appropriate when unemployment is localized or is a temporary phenomenon. By supporting and maintaining the individual's identity as a worker the nation's future labour supply is safeguarded. However, if unemployment is seen as a longer term phenomenon and if it is anticipated that many of the unemployed are unlikely to secure jobs in the foreseeable future, if ever, then help which is based on this assumption becomes a less obvious way forward.

The next chapter explores other strategies for helping the unemployed which include changing the organization in ways that make it easier for the unemployed to re-adjust to work and changing society in ways that will increase the demand for labour or in ways that will make it easier for the unemployed to adjust to their new status.

9 Helping the unemployed through measures designed to change the employing organization or society

'The girl who can't dance says the band can't play.'

Yiddish Proverb, 1949

Help for the unemployed can be categorized in terms of whether it involves changing the individual, changing the organization, or changing society. This chapter examines ways of helping the unemployed which focus on changing the organization or society, and underlines the importance of support, whether from supervisors, co-workers, the family or society at large, in the process of adjustment.

CHANGING THE ORGANIZATION

The emphasis of most efforts to help the unemployed has been to change the individual. However, in 1967 research on the Chicago JOBS NOW project found that it was impossible to predict the success of the hard core unemployed who entered the programme on the basis of individual differences. It was found that the only factor which differentiated, at statistically significant levels, the successful from the unsuccessful was the degree of support received within the immediate organizational context in which the individual was placed. The retention rate for high-support organizations was 82 per cent, while that for low-support organizations was merely 28 per cent (JOBS NOW Project 1967).

Friedlander and Greenberg (1969; 1971) examined the climate in which hard core unemployed workers were placed and the degree to which this climate was conducive to performance and retention. They conceptualized job climate as an interaction of personal factors, such as personality, values, and needs, and organizational properties, such as structure, supervisory practices, objectives, etc. This relationship emphasized the role of perception of organizational properties as an intervening variable. Particular attention was focused on the degree to which the individual perceived his work climate as supportive. Preliminary interviews with the hard core unemployed had indicated that three aspects of a supportive climate seem to be particularly salient. They were new worker treatment, support from peers, and support from supervisor. These were measured in the study by three specially constructed climate scales. Job performance was assessed through measures of job retention, work effectiveness (competence, congeniality, effort, and reliability), and work behaviour.

Two findings are of special interest here. One emerged from a comparison of the perception of the hard core unemployed and their supervisors of the work climate, and the other came from an analysis of the relationship between the supervisor's evaluation of the new employee and job retention. There was a very marked difference in the way the new employees and their supervisors perceived the work climate. Using a sample of twenty-four matched pairs of hard core unemployed and their respective supervisors in a variety of organizations it was found that the 'hard core' worker perceived the work climate as vastly less supportive than his supervisor. Turning to the supervisor's evaluation of new employees, a high negative relationship ($r = -0.60$) between the supervisor's evaluation of the employee as reliable and the number of weeks he worked (job retention) was found. Those who were rated as most reliable by their supervisors left after a very short duration and those who remained on the job tended to be the ones rated as less reliable by their supervisors. It was reliability rather than competence that seemed to be the most important variable. When the 'hard core' employee was present his work appeared to be comparable to that of other employees.

Friedlander and Greenberg suggested that this situation arose because the individual's prime method of coping with a work climate that he perceived to be highly unsupportive (and which his supervisor perceived to be supportive) was through his own unreliable behaviour by being late or absent. Those who were reliable on the job may have found the situation so intolerable that after only a short period they coped with the situation by leaving. Those who stayed coped with the unfavourable climate by being absent or late whenever the situation became unbearable.

Supervisory behaviour has long been recognized as an important variable influencing the performance of employees. It is not surprising, therefore, that a number of studies indicate that it can have an important effect on the performance and retention of the hard core unemployed. Whereas Friedlander and Greenberg found that supportiveness was related to reliability and retention, Goodale (1973) found that closeness of supervision was one of the most frequently reported sources of dissatisfaction. Both these findings appear to be consistent with Beatty's (1974) view that when the hard core unemployed perceive a supervisor as considerate or supportive they tend to perform more successfully, whereas when a supervisor is perceived as highly defining or structuring work activities they tend to perform less successfully. One might conclude, therefore, that organizations that hire the hard core unemployed should not only encourage supervisory styles that are initially supportive, but should also discourage styles that attempt to impose structure on individuals who may be unaccustomed to managing externally imposed demands.

Triandis et al. (1974) noted that analyses of culture shock suggest that people who find themselves in different cultures sometimes experience difficulty adapting. They experience disorientation and depression. Many habitual behaviours and responses fail to elicit reinforcements and they feel powerless to influence outcomes. Culture shock can be so punishing that 'escape from the field is the only rewarding response'. This is analogous to the new employee's unreliable behaviour observed by Friedlander and Greenberg.

Triandis et al. proposed that the development of institutions and personnel in the host environment who can recognize the visitor's need and help him adjust can be an important factor in reducing culture shock. They further propose that intercultural training that promotes change in both visitor and host, and which aims to make the behaviour of each participant in an interpersonal relationship more satisfying to the other member, can significantly reduce the visitor's propensity to leave the field. Triandis et al. (1974), following Kelley (1967), saw the major problem of interpersonal behaviour across cultures as one in which people make inappropriate attributions. The actor tends to see his own behaviour as being largely controlled by external factors, whereas the observer tends to see the actor's behaviour as being controlled by internal predispositions and personality factors. He believes that if the observer can be made more similar to the actor and give more weight to situational factors in his attributions about the cause of the actor's behaviour then interpersonal relations will improve. It is to achieve this end that Triandis *et al.* advocate a concentrated form of cognitive training known as a culture assimilator. The assimilator is a programmed learning sequence in which incidents of potential intercultural conflict are described and the trainee is asked to judge the relevance of various factors as causes of the incident. Usually a short paragraph is followed by a multi-choice format with four answers. Three might reflect attributions typically made by members of one culture (for example, supervisors) and the fourth might reflect a typical response from the other culture (new 'hard core' employee). In this example the trainee supervisor would select a response and then receive feedback on whether his answer reflected the attributions usually given by members of his or the other culture.

Triandis *et al.* suggest that it is unlikely that the cultural assimilator will work in those organizations where people do not receive reinforcement from members of their culture in response to 'appropriate' behaviours towards members of the other culture. In other words, they suggest that, in those organizations where supervisors are rewarded for good retention rates and for behaviour that promotes good retention, the assimilator approach is likely to be most useful. No follow up data on the success of the assimilator is given, but it is one of the few specific proposals for intercultural training in this context which is reported in the literature.

The individual who has been out of work for a considerable period of time may be faced as Triandis *et al.* suggest with a fairly major cultural transition. The transition is likely to be less successful when only one party, the new employee, is expected to change. This might be an appropriate model when a recruit is conscripted into the army because he does not have the freedom to leave; it might also be appropriate for a novice entering a monastery, because he might have the motivation to stay. However, the individual who has been out of work for a long time may have many reservations about making the transition from his unemployed state into the world of work. No one can force him to stay, and his motivation to succeed may not be very strong. Relatively small setbacks can be very discouraging. It is against this background that the need for a supportive work climate has to be assessed.

Reference was made in Chapter 8 to the relative success of the company-oriented training programme reported by Rosen and Turner and at least part of the success of this programme was attributed to the fact that training staff were able to intervene between trainees and first-time supervisors in order to clarify and resolve problems. In other words there was some flexibility in the organization's approach to the individual and the organization was prepared, within certain limits and on a temporary basis, to accommodate some of the special needs of the individual.

The importance of organizational as well as individual variables is also supported by a review of multi-firm studies reported by Goodman, Salipante, and Paransky (1973) in which they note that organizational commitment, company willingness to change policies and procedures, and realistic company expectations of the hard core unemployed are all related to retention rates.

It could be these kind of variables which have contributed to the success of the 'Work Experience on Employers' Premises' scheme organized for unemployed school leavers in the UK. The sponsoring organizations involved in this scheme seem to be committed to the project, sensitive to the needs of the young people who have little or no experience of the world of work, and are prepared to modify their normal policies and procedures in order to expose participants in the scheme to a variety of jobs and give them the training and special support they require.

It is relatively easy to organize activities designed to change the individual and it is also relatively easy for government agencies to be involved in the funding and management of such projects. Changing organizational variables can be considerably more difficult and the external agency may find it more difficult to influence and manage such changes. It should come as no surprise therefore to discover that most activities focus on changing the individual. None the less, there is sufficient evidence to indicate that a useful way forward may be to direct more effort towards designing activities to help the long-term unemployed re-establish themselves in the world of work, such as those proposed by Triandis *et al.* which pay attention to changing both individual and organizational variables.

CHANGING SOCIETY

A third manner in which some of the psychological problems associated with unemployment can be alleviated is through changes in society. Broadly speaking, these changes may come about in two ways: through an increase in demand for labour, or through a change in attitudes towards not working.

Attempts to tackle the problem of unemployment at the societal level have inescapable political implications. For example, a concentration upon helping people to adjust to unemployment is seen by some as a defeatist acceptance of economic trends that can be reversed. Conversely, failure to accept the need for such adjustment and to encourage instead the belief in the right to work and the possibility of full employment in the future, is seen by others as ostrich-like, and damaging in that it may create unrealistic expectations. These implications need to be borne in mind when considering the ways of helping the unemployed discussed below.

The demand for labour may be increased in a number of ways. The first, most often discussed way is to introduce measures to raise the overall level of economic activity. At the time of writing, however, the economic outlook is poor and most forecasters are predicting a long recession. We need, therefore, to turn our attention to those measures which can influence the demand for labour within the context of a stable or even a declining level of economic activity. One possibility is to look for ways of reversing the movement towards capital intensive methods of production. A fairly consistent trend in the developed economies over recent years has been a substitution of capital for labour, a trend which has received a fillip through recent advances in micro-technology. Employment subsidies which reduce the cost of labour to employers can retard this trend but the effect is only likely to be marginal, especially if a country's long-term competitive situation is to be safeguarded. For one country in isolation to abandon relatively cheap capital intensive methods of production in favour of more expensive labour intensive methods could lead to it being priced out of world markets. Employment subsidies have to be used with care. While they offer a useful means of helping employers cope with temporary problems and avoiding unnecessary redundancies over the short term they also present the danger of ossifying the economy and inhibiting necessary change over the long term.

Job creation programmes that generate new jobs in areas that are unlikely to hinder necessary structural changes in the economy can offer an attractive alternative means of increasing the demand for labour. The net cost of these schemes can be relatively small when the welfare payments participants would otherwise be entitled to are taken into account.

Measures can also be introduced which reduce the length of time it takes to fill vacancies, that is, to reduce frictional unemployment. This can be done through improving the flow of information between employers and job seekers, by providing occupational guidance that will direct job seekers in new directions, and by improving the job search skills of individual job seekers. Geographical mis-matches between the supply and demand for labour can also be smoothed through the provision of grants and other help to facilitate the free movement of labour.

In addition to adopting measures aimed at raising the demand for labour, it is possible to focus attention on re-directing this demand so that certain sections of the potential work force find it easier to obtain employment. In the UK the Job Release Scheme provides encouragement to some older workers to retire early in order to create an opportunity for younger workers who are without jobs. Measures like the Youth Opportunity Scheme, in addition to creating new jobs, probably make the employment of younger rather than older workers more attractive to employers. Special measures can also discriminate in favour of other groups such as the disabled.

More people can be drawn into the labour force if part-time working and other work-sharing schemes are introduced. While little progress seems to have been made down this particular road there has been pressure to reduce overtime working, to shorten the working week, introduce longer holidays, and the like. Another possibility is to lower the retirement age.

All these measures assume that every effort should be made to re-employ all those bereft of work. It was noted at the beginning of Chapter 8 that the unemployed tend to be seen as outsiders and deviants. The unemployed male is a prime target for censure because of his failure to fulfil his role of family provider. In a culture which prizes individualism and autonomy he can also be seen as a failure when he has to seek help. Many countries adopt welfare policies which cast the unemployed in the role of 'lazy scrounger' who has to be encouraged to throw off his sloth. While this may be a fair description of some of the unemployed (Maclean 1977), there are signs that many people continue to work even when this brings little or no economic advantage.

Occasionally, but with increasing frequency, the call can be heard for a different approach for dealing with those out of work. One which rewards rather than discriminates against the unemployed. It has been suggested that those who are willing not to work should be compensated or rewarded in order to free jobs and create opportunities for those who want to work. Such an approach attributes to the unemployed a very different status from that which they are accorded at present. While this approach may appear attractive it is very counter to the culture of our society, a society in which the unemployed tend to be seen as second-class citizens, and the state of unemployment is seen as the source of many social problems. Indeed, there can be little doubt that at the moment delinquency, racial unrest and many other social problems are exacerbated by unemployment. It may well be that 'the devil finds work for idle hands', but need idleness and purposelessness be a consequence of unemployment? Maybe the solution is to find alternatives to employment, rather than to promote the work ethic and keep alive the promise of jobs when the supply of labour is greatly in excess of demand and when it is likely to remain so for the foreseeable future. If the imbalance in the labour market is temporary, yet another phase in a regular cycle to be followed by a period of full employment, then the argument for changing social attitudes to unemployment may be purely academic. If, on the other hand, we are as many predict on the threshold of a long period of unemployment, it may well be time to consider whether society should shift the emphasis away from helping *all* the unemployed prepare for and regain employment towards offering some of them, where appropriate, help to accept and adjust to their new-found status.

There is evidence that social support can help the individual cope with stressful events (see Cobb 1976; and Pinneau 1975). Support is one of the main purposes of the many mutual help organizations that have proliferated in an attempt to help people manage life crises. There is evidence, however, that many people who are unemployed are sadly lacking in such support, especially if they have been unemployed for some time. This lack of support runs throughout society and can even be found in the heart of the nuclear family. Take the example of a male worker who has recently experienced redundancy. In the early phases of unemployment, the usual rhythm of family life tends to be maintained. The (unemployed) father continues to spend time outside the home seeking work. Social activities seem to be maintained and, according to Bakke (1960), the division of labour in the home is altered very little. Any changes in relationships within the family during this period are usually for the better. The father sees more of young children and the bonds between them are often strengthened. The wife usually accepts her husband's plight and supports him both within the home and outside.

As the period of unemployment extends, the situation as experienced by the unemployed worker and his family slowly begins to change. Savings are eroded, financial problems present themselves, and the necessity for increasingly severe adjustments becomes obvious. It is at this stage that pressures begin to build up within the family. The wife may begin to provide an alternative source of income by seeking outside work for the first time, or by increasing the time she devotes to paid employment. This results in a redivision of labour within the home. The wife delegates domestic chores to the children and begins to assume duties previously reserved for the husband. Bakke reports that she begins to assume a greater degree of responsibility for management and for distributing the available income. He also notes that the husband, discouraged and tired out by his search for work, often takes this excuse to withdraw from his parental responsibilities in other respects, so that the decisions as to the activities of the several members of the family descend upon the wife and mother. Consequently the husband's status begins to decline in the eyes of both his wife and children. This is sometimes accompanied by older children, who contribute to the family's income, demanding more freedom in view of their increased importance as family providers.

Crises become more frequent as opportunities for conflict between husband and wife and father and children increase. Family life becomes less satisfying for all and little energy is devoted to forward planning. None the less, Bakke reports that to the outside world the family, and particularly the wife, attempt to provide a united and loyal front. Eventually, however, this may be eroded. The wife may become bitter, question the sincerity of her husband's search for work and express the suspicion that he is loafing. Finally, she may stop defending the father from the criticisms of the children and even criticize him outside the home. At this point there is little or no support for the father. He is alone within the family and has to deal with his problem as best he can.

Loss of job is unlike change of job in that it is often associated with social isolation. For many their work role is a very important social role and is linked with membership of various work-related role sets. Unemployment disqualifies the individual from membership of these role sets. Thus, not only is it associated with loss of authority within the family and status in the community but also with loss of many work-related contacts.

Gore (1974; 1978) investigated the influences of social support in ameliorating the consequences of job loss. Following the close down of two plants, 100 married men who had been stably employed were interviewed at five points over a two-year period. Social support was measured by a 13-item index covering the extent of supportive and affiliative relations with wife, friends, and relatives. Of the terminees 46 per cent started a new job shortly after termination, while the rest took two or three months longer. A small group (approximately 12 per cent of the sample) were still unemployed after six months. No differences were found between the supported and unsupported with respect to length of unemployment or actual economic deprivation, but social support was found to moderate the impact of the objective unemployment experience. While unemployed, the unsupported evidenced a stronger sense of economic deprivation, strikingly elevated cholesterol levels at termination, intense negative feelings towards the trade union, elevated levels of illness and illness complaining, and were consistently depressed. The terminees experiencing least strain were those who were well supported or who experienced little if any unemployment.

Family counselling is one means of helping the unemployed and his or her family adjust to their new situation. Tauss (1976) suggests that both wife and husband may need help when the husband is made redundant and describes how many husbands experience a profound sense of inadequacy, failure, and devaluation of their masculine role when faced with their inability to provide a livelihood in support of their family. As noted above, their distress may be magnified when they are forced to turn the role of financial provider over to their wives. Their wives, simultaneously, may experience the uncertainty of reorganizing their entire schedule of activities in order to exchange many roles with their husbands. Both husband and wife may face an unprecedented threat to their basic security which somehow seems to create demands which invade every aspect of life. Tauss sees the family counsellor's role in these circumstances as assisting couples to examine the situation objectively and find appropriate, constructive means of dealing with the problems presented. Children, other relatives, close friends, and neighbours may also have a role to play. Since these persons can be highly influential in the success or failure of a transition between husband and wife, Tauss believes that they may have to be included in the counselling process.

Community support for the unemployed can take many forms. The British Council of Churches, in the booklet *Work or What?* describes a range of activities which range from creative protest to group and individual counselling. Many community organizations other than the church are involved, especially with helping school leavers cope with the problem of unemployment. None the less, helping the unemployed, and those close to them, adjust and accept the situation and establish new non-work goals and purposes in life seems to receive considerably less attention than attempts to keep alive the work ethic and prepare the unemployed to resume the role of worker.

Strategies to facilitate this transition from unemployed to employed, which have been discussed in this and the previous chapter, include changing the individual to make him or her more employable, or to increase his or her motivation and ability to seek and secure work. Achieving this kind of change with the recently unemployed is sometimes helped by the fact that many unemployed often attribute blame for their predicament to themselves and believe that the remedy is for them to change. Alternative strategies include helping the unemployed person negotiate the transition into work by making the organization more accommodating and, where the individual has been unemployed for some time, by helping the individual anticipate the work culture they will encounter. A final set of strategies aim to ease the transition by increasing the supply of jobs.

At the time of writing the supply of jobs is actually falling and within this context many of the measures discussed in this chapter merely increase the chances of some people securing employment at the expense of others. If the objective of helping the unemployed is to keep alive the work ethic then these measures may be successful. If, on the other hand, it is to ameliorate the consequence of unemployment for the individual then how successful they will be is more difficult to assess. There has been little attempt to measure this. There is the possibility that attempts to help the individual secure employment, if unsuccessful, may actually worsen the consequences of unemployment for that person. Furthermore, the consequences of adopting measures which bolster the cultural norm (that which demands that the unemployed find work as quickly as possible), have not been assessed for the vast majority of the unemployed who have not been involved in these measures and, therefore, have not had their competitive edge sharpened for the fight for work.

It is not within the scope of this discussion to recommend specific ways forward. Our aim has been to promote a better understanding of the unemployed, and to contribute to the debate on how to ameliorate the effects of unemployment. More needs to be done and more can be done. We hope that what we have written here will be of help to all – family, friends, members of the helping professions, politicians, administrators, and others – who are concerned about unemployment.

References

ADLER, A. (1931) *What Life Should Mean to You.* New York: Blue Books.

ADLER, A. (1964) *Social Interest: A Challenge to Mankind.* New York: Capricorn Books.

ALFANO, A. M. (1973) A Scale to Measure Attitudes Toward Working. *Journal of Vocational Behaviour* 3: 329–33.

ALLEN, C. A. (1975) Life Planning: Its Purpose and Position in the Human Potential Movement. Unpublished MA thesis, Department of Management Studies, University of Leeds.

ALLERHAND, M. E., FRIEDLANDER, F., MALONE, J. E., MEDOW, H., and ROSENBERG, M. (1969) *A Study of the Impact and Effectiveness of the Comprehensive Manpower Project of Cleveland (AIM-JOBS).* Cleveland, Ohio: AIM Research Project, Office of Policy, Evaluation and Research, US Department of Labor. Contract No. 41-7-002.37.

ANGYAL, A. (1965) *Neurosis and Treatment: Holistic Theory.* New York: John Wiley.

ARGYRIS, C. (1957) *Personality and Organization.* New York: Harper & Row.

AYLLON, T. and AZRIN, N. H. (1968) *The Token Economy: A Motivation System for Therapy and Rehabilitation.* New York: Appleton-Century-Crofts.

BAKKE, E. W. (1933) *The Unemployed Man.* Nisbett.

BAKKE, E. W. (1940a) *Citizens Without Work.* New Haven, Conn.: Yale University Press.

BAKKE, E. W. (1940b) *The Unemployed Worker.* New Haven, Conn.: Yale University Press.

BAKKE, E. W. (1960) The Cycle of Adjustment to Unemployment. In N. W. Bell and E. F. Vogal (eds) *A Modern Introduction to the Family.* New York: Free Press.

BEATTY, R. W. (1974) Supervisory Behaviour Related to Job Success of Hard-core Unemployed over a Two-year Period. *Journal of Applied Psychology* 59(1): 38–42.

BECKER, H. (1964) *Personal Change in Adult Life*. Sociometry.

BERGER, P. and LUCKMANN, T. (1967) *The Social Construction of Reality*. Harmondsworth: Penguin Books.

BOLLES, R. (1978) *The Three Boxes of Life*. Berkeley, Calif.: Ten Speed Press.

BOLLES, R. (1980) *What Color is Your Parachute?* Berkeley, Calif.: Ten Speed Press.

BOWSER, S. W., SHERMAN, G., and WHISLER, R. H. (1974) An Action-research Approach to Central City Unemployment. *Journal of Vocational Behaviour* 4(1): 115–24.

BREED, W. (1963) Occupational Mobility and Suicide among White Males. *American Journal of Sociology* 28(2): 179–88.

BRIAR, K. H. (1977) The Effect of Long-term Unemployment on Workers and Their Families. *Dissertation Abstracts International* (March) 37(9-A): 6062.

BUGLASS, D. and HORTON, J. (1974) The Repetition of Parasuicide: A Comparison of Three Cohorts. *British Journal of Psychiatry* 125: 168–74.

CHAPLIN, J. P. and KRAWIEC, T. S. (1968) *Systems and Theories of Psychology*. London: Holt, Rinehart & Winston.

COBB, S. (1976) Social Support as a Moderator of Life Stress. *Psychosomatic Medicine* 38: 300–14.

COBB, S., BROOKS, G. W., KASL, S. V., and CONNELLY, W. E. (1966) The Health of People Changing Jobs: A Description of a Longitudinal Study. *American Journal of Public Health* 56: 1476–481.

COBB, S., MCFARLAND, D., KASL, S. V. and BROOKS, G. W. (1970) *On the Relationship among Variables in a Longitudinal Study of People Changing Jobs*. Proceedings of the 5th International Scientific Meeting of the International Epidemiological Association. Belgrade: Savremena Administracija Publishing House.

COHEN, A. R. and ZIMBARDO, P. G. (1962) An Experiment in Avoidance Motivation. In J. W. Behm and A. R. Cohen (eds) *Explorations in Cognitive Dissonance*. New York: John Wiley.

COOLEY, G. M. (1922) *Human Nature and Social Order*. New York: Scribner.

CRAWFORD, M. (1971) Retirement and Disengagement. *Human Relations* 24(3): 225–78.

CULL, J. G. and HARDY, R. W. (1973) *Rehabilitation of the Urban Disadvantaged*. Springfield, Ill.: Charles C. Thomas.

DANIEL, W. W. (1974) *A National Survey of the Unemployed.* PEP **XL**, Broadsheet No. 546.

DUBIN, R. (1956) Industrial Workers' Worlds: A Study of the 'Central Life Interests' of Industrial Workers. *Social Problems* **3**: 131–42.

DURKHEIM, E. (1933) *The Division of Labour in Society.* New York: Free Press.

DURKHEIM, E. (1952) *Suicide: A Study in Sociology.* London: Routledge & Kegan Paul.

DYER, W. G. (1956) The Interlocking of Work and Family Social Systems among Lower Occupational Families. *Social Forces* **34**(1): 230–33.

EISENBERG, P. and LAZARSFELD, P. F. (1938) The Psychological Effects of Unemployment. *Psychological Bulletin* **XXXV**: 358–90.

ELLIS, A. (1973a) Rational-emotive Therapy. In R. Corsini (ed.) *Current Psychotherapies.* Itasca, Ill.: Peacock.

ELLIS, A. (1973b) *Humanistic Psychotherapy: The Rational-Emotive Approach.* New York: Julian Press.

FAUNCE, W. (1968) *Problems of an Industrial Society.* New York: McGraw-Hill.

FESTINGER, L. (1957) *A Theory of Cognitive Dissonance.* Evanston, Ill.: Row, Peterson.

FINEMAN, S. (1979) A Psychological Model of Stress and Its Application to Managerial Unemployment. *Human Relations* **32**: 323–45.

FRANK, H. H. (1969) *On the Job Training for Minorities: An Internal Study.* Unpublished doctoral thesis, University of California, Los Angeles.

FRENCH, J. R. P. and KAHN, R. L. (1962) A Programmatic Approach to Studying the Industrial Environment and Mental Health. *Journal of Social Issues* **18**(3): 1–47.

FRIEDLANDER, F. and GREENBERG, S. (1969) Work Climate as Related to the Performance and Retention of Hard-core Unemployed Workers. *Proceedings of the 77th Annual Convention of the American By. Association* **4** (Pt 2): 607–08.

FRIEDLANDER, F. and GREENBERG, S. (1971) Effect of Job Attitudes, Training and Organization Climate on Performance of the Hard-core Unemployed. *Journal of Applied Psychology* **55**(4): 287–95.

FULTON, R. and FULTON, J. (1972) Anticipatory Grief. In B.

Schoenberg et al. (eds) *Psychosocial Aspects of Terminal Care.* New York: Columbia University Press.

GIBBS, J. and MARTIN, W. (1964) *Status Integration and Suicide.* Eugene, Ore.: University of Oregon Press.

GINSBERG et al. (1970) The Unemployed. Quoted in C. Sofer, *Men in Mid-career.* Cambridge: Cambridge University Press.

GOFFMAN, E. (1952) On Cooling the Mark Out. *Psychiatry* **15**(4): 451–63.

GOFFMAN, E. (1955) On Face Work. *Psychiatry* **18**: 213–31.

GOLDING, P. and MIDDLETON, S. (1978) Why is the Press so Obsessed with Welfare Scroungers? *New Society* (26 October).

GOODALE, J. G. (1973) Effects of Personal Background and Training on Work Values of the Hard-core Unemployed. *Journal of Applied Psychology* (February) **57**(1): 1–9.

GOODMAN, P. and SALIPANTE, P. (1976) Organizational Rewards and Retention of the Hard-core Unemployed. *Journal of Applied Psychology* (February) **61**(1): 12–21.

GOODMAN, P. S., SALIPANTE, P., and PARANSKY, H. (1973) Hiring Training and Retraining the Hard-core Unemployed: A Selected Review. *Journal of Applied Psychology* (August) **58**(1): 23–33.

GORE, S. (1974) The Influence of Social Support and Related Variables in Ameliorating the Consequences of Job Loss. PhD thesis, University of Pennsylvania. *Dissertation Abstracts International* **38** (8-A, Pt 2): 5330–331.

GORE, S. (1978) The Effects of Social Support in Moderating the Health Consequences of Unemployment. *Journal of Health and Social Behaviour* (June) **19**(2): 157–65.

GOULD, T. and KENYON, J. (1972) *Stories from the Dole Queue.* London: Temple Smith.

GOULDNER, A. W. (1968) Cosmopolitans and Locals. In B. G. Glaser (ed.) *Organizational Careers.* Chicago: Aldine.

GRIFFITHS, R., HODGSON, R., and HALLAM, R. (1974) Structured Interview for the Assessment of Work Related Attitudes in Psychiatric Patients: Preliminary Findings. *Psychological Medicine* **4**: 326–33.

HARRISON, R. (1976) The Demoralising Experience of Prolonged Unemployment. *Department of Employment Gazette* (April): 339–48.

HARTLAGE, L. C. and JOHNSON, R. P. (1971) Developing Work Behaviour in the Hard-core Unemployed with Video Play Back. *Perceptual and Motor Skills* (December) **33**(3, Pt 2): 1343–346.

HARTLEY, J. and COOPER, C. L. (1978) Managers Without Organizations. *Management Bibliographies and Reviews* 4: 58–67.

HARTMANN, P. (1972) A Study of Attitudes in Industrial Rehabilitation. *Occupational Psychology* 46(2): 87–97.

HENDRICK, I. (1943a) The Work and Pleasure Principle. *Psychoanalytic Quarterly* 12: 311–29.

HENDRICK, I. (1943b) The Discussion of the Instinct to Master. *Psychoanalytic Quarterly* 12: 516–65.

HERRON, F. (1975) *Labour Market in Crisis*. London: Macmillan.

HERZBERG, F., MAUSNER, B., PETERSON, R. O., and CAPWELL, D. F. (1957) *Job Attitudes: Review of Research and Opinion*. Pittsburgh, Pa.: Psychological Services of Pittsburgh.

HILL, J. (1977) The Social and Psychological Impact of Unemployment: A Pilot Study. *Tavistock Institute of Human Relations* No. 2T: 74.

HILL, J. (1978) The Psychological Impact of Unemployment. *New Society* (19 January).

HODGSON, J. D. and BRENNER, M. H. (1968) Successful Experience: Training Hard-core Unemployed. *Harvard Business Review* 46: 148–56.

HOLMES, T. H. and MASUDA, M. (1973) Life Change and Illness Susceptibility. In J. P. Scott and E. C. Senay (eds) *Separation and Depression: Clinical and Research Aspects*. Washington, DC: AAAS.

HOLMES, T. H. and RAHE, R. H. (1967) The Social Readjustment Rating Scale. *Journal of Psychosomatic Research* 11: 213–18.

HOPSON, B. (1976) Personal Re-evaluation: A Method for Individual Goal-setting. In J. Adams, J. Hayes, and B. Hopson, *Transition*. London: Martin Robertson.

HOPSON, B. and ADAMS, J. (1976) Towards an Understanding of Transition: Defining some Boundaries of Transition Dynamics. In J. Adams, J. Hayes, and B. Hopson, *Transition*. London: Martin Robertson.

HOUSE, J. S. (1974) Effects of Occupational Stress on Physical Health. In J. O'Toole (ed.) *Work and the Quality of Life*. Cambridge, Mass.: MIT Press.

HUTSON, R. H. and SMITH, J. R. (1969) A Community Wide Approach to Training the Hard-core. *Personnel Training* 48(6): 428–33.

HYMAN, H. H. (1979) The Effects of Unemployment: A Neglected Problem in Modern Social Research. In R. K. Merton (ed.)

Qualitative and Quantitative Social Research. New York: Free Press.

JACO, F. G. (1960) *The Social Epidemiology of Mental Disorders – A Psychiatric Survey of Texas*. New York: Russell Sage Foundation.

JAHODA, M. (1970) Notes on Work. *Psychoanalysis – A General Psychology*, quoted in C. Sofer *Men in Mid-career*. Cambridge: Cambridge University Press.

JAHODA, M. (1979) The Impact of Unemployment in the 1930s and 1970s. *Bulletin of the British Psychological Society* **32**: 309–14.

Jobs Now Project (1967) Status Rep. No. 3. Chicago, Ill.

JONES, M. (1972) *Life on the Dole*. London: Davis Poynter.

Just the Job (1979) Westward Television and National Extension College Trust.

KAHN, R. L. and FRENCH, J. R. P. (1970) Status Conflict: Two Themes in the Study of Stress. In J. E. McGrath (ed.) *Social and Psychological Factors in Stress*. New York: Holt, Rinehart & Winston.

KASL, S. and COBB, S. (1970) Blood Pressure Changes in Men Undergoing Job Loss: A Preliminary Report. *Psychosomatic Medicine* **32**: 19–38.

KASL, S. and COBB, S. (1971) Some Physical and Mental Health Effects of Job Loss. *Pakistan Medical Forum* (April) **vi**(4): 95–106.

KASL, S., COBB, S., and GORE, S. (1972) Changes in Reported Illness and Illness Behaviour Related to Termination of Employment: A Preliminary Report. *International Journal of Epidemiology* **1**: 111–18.

KASL, S., GORE, S., and COBB, S. (1975) The Experience of Losing a Job: Reported Changes in Health Symptoms and Illness Behaviour. *Psychosomatic Medicine* (March) **37**(2): 106–22.

KATZ, D. and KAHN, R. L. (1978) *The Social Psychology of Organizations*. 2nd ed. New York: John Wiley.

KELLEY, H. H. (1967) Attribution Theory in Social Psychology. In D. Levine (ed.) *Nebraska Symposium on Motivation*. Lincoln, Nebr.: University of Nebraska Press.

KELLY, G. (1980) *A Study of the Manager's Orientation Towards the Transition from Work to Retirement*. Unpublished PhD thesis, University of Leeds.

KIRCHNER, W. K. and LUCAS, J. A. (1972) Hard-core in Training:

Who Makes It? *Training and Development Journal* (May) **26**(5): 34–7.

LEWIN, K. (1935) *A Dynamic Theory of Personality*. New York: McGraw-Hill.

LEWIN, K. (1938) *The Conceptual Representation and the Measurement of Psychological Forces*. Durham, NC: Duke University Press.

LITTLE, C. B. (1976) Technical-Professional Unemployment: Middle-class Adaptability to Personal Crisis. *Sociological Quarterly* **17**(2): 262–74.

LYTHGOE, P. (1979) The Social Security Snowball. *The Media Reporter* **3**(1).

MCCALL, G. J. and SIMMONS, J. L. (1966) *Identities and Interactions*. London: Collier-Macmillan.

MACLEAN, M. E. (1977) Learning Theory and Chronic Welfare Dependency: A Hypothesis of Etiological and Contingency Relationships. *Journal of Behaviour Therapy and Experimental Psychiatry* **8**(3): 255–59.

MANPOWER SERVICES COMMISSION (1979) *Review of the First Year of Special Programmes*.

MARGOLIS, B. L. and KROES, W. H. (1974) Work and the Health of Man. In J. O'Toole (ed.) *Work and the Quality of Life*. Cambridge, Mass.: MIT Press.

MARSDEN, D. and DUFF, E. (1975) *Workless: Some Unemployed Men and Their Families*. Harmondsworth: Penguin Books.

MEAD, G. H. (1934) *Self*, excerpts from *Mind, Self and Society*. Reprinted in K. Thompson and J. Tunstall (eds) (1971) *Sociological Perspectives*. Harmondsworth: Penguin Books.

MERTON, R. K. (1940) Bureaucratic Structure and Personality. *Social Forces* No. 18: 560–68.

MERTON, R. K. (1968) *Role Sets*, excerpts from *Social Theory and Social Structure*. Reprinted in K. Thompson and J. Tunstall (eds) (1971) *Sociological Perspectives*. Harmondsworth: Penguin Books.

MOORE, P. (1980) Counter Culture in a Social Security Office. *New Society* (10 July).

MORGAN, R. and CHEADLE, A. J. (1975) Unemployment Impedes Resettlement. *Social Psychiatry* **10**: 63–67.

MORIYAMA, I. M., KRUEGER, D. E., and STAMLER, J. (1971) *Cardiovascular Diseases in the United States*. Cambridge, Mass.: Harvard University Press.

MORSE, N. C. and WEISS, R. S. (1955) The Function and Meaning of Work and the Job. *American Sociological Review* **20**: 191–95.

NALLY, M. (1979) Jobless Crisis for Bradford Asians. *Sunday Observer* (10 June).

NEFF, W. S. (1968) *Work and Human Behaviour*. New York: Atherton Press.

NEWMAN, J. F., WHITTEMORE, K. R., and NEWMAN, H. G. (1973) Women in the Labour Force. *Social Problems* **21**(2): 220–30.

NUTMAN, P. N. S. (1977) The Mediation of Social Security. *The Media Reporter* **1**: 3.

O'LEARY, V. E. (1972) The Hawthorne Effect in Reverse: Trainee Orientation for the Hard-core Unemployed Woman. *Journal of Applied Psychology* (December) **56**(6): 491–94.

ORWELL, G. (1975) *The Road to Wigan Pier*. Harmondsworth: Penguin Books.

ORZACK, L. H. (1959) Work as a 'Central Life Interest' of Professionals. *Social Problems* **7**: 125–32.

O'TOOLE, J. (ed.) (1974) *Work and the Quality of Life*. Cambridge, Mass: MIT Press.

PARKES, C. M. (1971) Psycho-social Transitions: A Field for Study. *Social Science and Medicine* **5**: 101–15.

PARKES, C. M. (1972) *Bereavement: Studies of Grief in Adult Life*. London: Tavistock Publications.

PERUCCI, R. and GERSTL, J. E. (1969) *Profession Without Community: Engineers in American Society*. New York: Random House.

PILGRIM TRUST (1968) *Men Without Work*. Cambridge: Cambridge University Press.

PINNEAU, S. R. (1975) *Effects of Social Support on Psychological and Physiological Strains*. PhD thesis, University of Michigan.

POWELL, D. H. (1973) The Effects of Job Strategy Seminars Upon Unemployed Engineers and Scientists. *Journal of Social Psychology* (October) **91**(1): 165–66.

PURCELL, T. V. and WEBSTER, R. (1969) 196 Men Find a Chance. In P. Doeringer (ed.) *Programs to Employ the Disadvantaged*. Englewood Cliffs, NJ: Prentice-Hall.

QUINN, R., FINE, B., and LEVITIN, T. (1970) *Turnover and Training: A Social-psychological Study of Disadvantaged Workers*. Unpublished paper, Survey Research Centre, University of Michigan.

RAINWATER, L. (1974) Work, Well-being and Family Life. In J. O'Toole (ed.) *Work and the Quality of Life*. Cambridge, Mass.: MIT Press.

ROSEN, H. and TURNER, J. (1971) Effectiveness of Two Orientation Approaches to Hard-core Unemployed Turnover and Absenteeism. *Journal of Applied Psychology* (August) **55**(4): 296–301.

ROTTER, J. B. (1954) *Social Learning and Clinical Psychology*. Englewood Cliffs, NJ: Prentice-Hall.

SAINSBURY, P. (1955) *Suicide in London*. London: Chapman & Hall.

SALEH, S. O. and OTIS, J. L. (1963) Sources of Job Satisfaction and their Effects on Attitudes to Retirement. *Journal of Industrial Psychology* **1**: 101–06.

SALIPANTE, P. and GOODMAN, P. (1976) Training, Counselling and Retention of the Hard-core Unemployed. *Journal of Applied Psychology* (February) **61**(1): 1–11.

SANDLER, J. and TURNER, W. L. (1973) Vocational Preparation of the Hard-core Unemployed: The Token Economy. *Rehabilitation Counselling Bulletin* (December) **17**(2): 79–91.

SATHYVATHI, K. (1977) Suicides among Unemployed Persons in Bangalore. *Indian Journal of Social Work* (January) **37**(4): 385–92.

SCHAFFER, K. F. (1976) Evaluating Job Satisfaction and Success for Emotionally Maladjusted Men. *Journal of Vocational Behaviour* **9**: 329–35.

SCHLACHET, P. J. (1962) The Effects of Dissonance Arousal on the Recall of Failure Stimuli. *Journal of Personality* **30**.

SCHLIEN, T. (1963) Phenomenology and Personality. In J. M. Wepman and R. W. Heine (eds) *Concepts of Personality*. Chicago: Aldine Press.

SCHWARZ, B. (1974) Waiting, Exchange and Power: The Distribution of Time in Social Systems. *American Journal of Sociology* **79**: 841–87.

SCHWEITZER, S. O. and SMITH, R. E. (1974) The Persistence of the Discouraged Worker Effect. *Industrial and Labour Relations Review* **27**(2): 249–60.

SEEMAN, M. (1963) Alienation and Social Learning in a Reformatory. *American Journal of Sociology* **56**: 270–84.

SELIGMAN, M. E. P. (1975) *Helplessness*. San Francisco: W. H. Freeman.

SELLS, S. B. (1969) *The Definition and Measurement of Mental*

Health. PHS Publication No. 1873. Washington, DC: US Government Printing Office.

SHANDY, G. A. and KUC, S. G. (1977) Preparing the Hard-core Disadvantaged for Employment; Social Skills Orientation Course: An Evaluation. *Canadian Journal of Criminology* (July) **19**(3): 303–09.

SHAPIRO, B. A. (1978) Employment and Self Esteem: An Evaluation of the Cambridge Job Factory, a Manpower Programme under the Comprehensive Employment Training Act. *Dissertation Abstracts International* (September) **39**(3-A): 1852.

SHEPPARD, H. L. and BELITSKY, A. H. (1966) *The Job Hunt: Job-seeking Behaviour of Unemployed Workers in a Local Economy.* Baltimore, Md: Johns Hopkins Press.

SHIMIN, S. (1966) Concepts of Work. *Occupational Psychology* **40**: 195–201.

SINFIELD, A. (1970) Poor and Out of Work in Shields. In P. Townsend (ed.) *The Concept of Poverty.* London: Heinemann.

SOFER, C. (1970) *Men in Mid-career.* Cambridge: Cambridge University Press.

SPALT, L. (1977) Occupational Characteristics in Affective Disorders. *Diseases of the Nervous System* **38** (Pt 7): 548–52.

STONE, R. C. and SCHLAMP, F. T. (1971) *Welfare and Working Fathers.* Lexington, Mass.: D. C. Heath.

STRANGE, W. G. (1978) Job Loss: A Psycho-social Study of Worker Reactions to a Plant Closing in a Company Town in South Appalachia. *Dissertation Abstracts International* (June) **38** (12-B).

SUPER, D. (1953) A Theory of Vocational Development. *American Psychologist* **8**: 185–90.

SUSSER, M. (1967) Causes of Peptic Ulcer: A Selective Epidemiologic Review. *Journal of Chronic Diseases* **20**: 435–56.

SWANK, R. L. and MARCHAND, E. (1946) Combat Neurosis, Development of Combat Exhaustion. *Archives of Neurology and Psychiatry* **LV**: 236.

TAUSS, V. (1976) Working Wife – House Husband: Implications for Counselling. *Journal of Family Counselling* **4**(2): 52–55.

TEAHAN, J. E. (1969) Future Time Perspective and Job Success. In supplement to H. Rosen, *A Group Oriented Approach for Facilitating the Work Adjustment of the Hard-core Unemployed.* Final Report, US Dept of Labor. Washington, DC: US Government Printing Office.

TIFFANY, D. W., COWAN, J. R., and TIFFANY, P. M. (1970) *The Unemployed: A Social-psychological Portrait*. Englewood Cliffs, NJ: Prentice-Hall.

TILGHER, A. (1958) *Work Through the Ages*. Chicago: Henry Regenery.

TOLMAN, E. C. (1932) *Purposive Behaviour in Animals and Men*. New York: Appleton-Century.

TOWNSEND, P. (1979) *Poverty in the United Kingdom*. Harmondsworth: Penguin Books.

TRIANDIS, H. C. (1974) Culture Training, Cognitive Complexity and Interpersonal Attitudes. In R. W. Brislin, S. Bochner, and W. J. Lonner (eds) *Cross-cultural Perspectives and Learning* Vol. 1. Beverley Hills, Calif.: Sage.

TRIANDIS, H. C., FELDMAN, J. M., WELDON, D., and HARVEY, W. M. (1974) Designing Pre-employment Training for the Hard to Employ: A Cross-cultural Psychological Approach. *Journal of Applied Psychology* (December) **59**(6): 687–93.

TYLER, L. (1961) *The Work of the Counsellor*. New York: Appleton-Century-Crofts.

VROOM, V. (1964) *Work and Motivation*. New York: John Wiley.

WALBRAN, B., MACMAHON, B., and BAILEY, A. E. (1965). Suicide and Unemployment in Pennsylvania 1954–1961. *Archives of Environmental Health* (10 January): 11–15.

WARR, P. and LOVATT, J. (1977) Retraining and Other Factors Associated with Job Finding After Redundancy. *Journal of Occupational Psychology* (June) **50**(2): 67–84.

WEBER, M. (1930) *The Protestant Ethic and the Spirit of Capitalism*. London: Allen & Unwin.

WILLIAMS, R. (1976) *Keywords: A Vocabulary of Culture and Society*. London: Fontana Books.

WILSON, L. T., BERRY, K. L., and MISKIMINS, R. W. (1969) An Assessment of the Characteristics Related to Vocational Success Among Restored Psychiatric Patients. *Vocational Guidance Quarterly* **5**: 110–14.

Work or What? A Christian Examination of the Employment Crisis (1977) London: CIO Publishing.

Name index

Subject index